AF791383

Lectures on History of Manipur

Lectures on History of Manipur

GANGMUMEI KAMEI

AKANSHA PUBLISHING HOUSE
NEW DELHI • GUWAHATI • VISAKHAPATNAM

AKANSHA PUBLISHING HOUSE
4649-B/21, Ansari Road
Daryaganj, New Delhi-110002
Phones: 23268193, 09435116718
Email: ektabooks@yahoo.com
visit us: www.akanshapublishinghouse.com

Lectures on History of Manipur

© Indian Institute of Advanced Study, Shimla

First Published 2012
Reprint 2026

ISBN 978-81-8370-311-6

[All rights reserved. No part of this publication may be reproduced or transmitted, in any form or by any means, without prior permission of the author. Any person who does any unauthorised act in relation to this publication may be liable to criminal prosecution and civil claims for damages.]

PRINTED IN INDIA

Published by Akansha Publishing House, New Delhi-110002 and printed at Harmain Offset Printers, Delhi.

Dedicated to

Late Pandit *N. KHELCHANDRA SINGH,*

Padmashree

Antiquarian, Historian and Scholar

Extraordinary of Manipur

Contents

Preface

"The Lectures on the History of Manipur" is a collection of four lectures which I delivered at the Indian Institute of Advanced Study at Shimla. I am grateful to Professor Peter de Souza, Director of the Institute for giving me the honour of being a National Fellow at the Institute. He also kindly gave the permission to me and the publisher to publish the lectures on the condition that the copyright of these lectures is vested in the Indian Institute of Advanced Study. The four lectures are not part of the monograph I am writing as an academic assignment of the National fellowship. I enjoyed a wonderful infrastructure and beautiful academic atmosphere at the Institute during my residence. I got an extremely useful interaction with Professor Peter de Souza, my colleagues, Professor M. Palat and Professor Ghanshyam Shah who are also National Fellows in the preparation of the lectures. I owe a lot to Professor Shah for his views and suggestions on the themes of the lectures. The themes of the lectures are Historiography, Feudalism, Colonialism and Ethno nationalism of Manipur. I have the great pleasure to dedicate this humble work to the sweet memory of late Pandit N. Khelchandra Singh, a talking encyclopaedia of Manipur during his life time.

I acknowledge the help of Mr. S.P. Thakur, IAS, Secretary of the Institute and Dr. D. Sen of the Administrative and Publication Section given to me in my academic works. I also got help from Professor N. Joykumar Singh and Dr. C. Mathew of History Department, Manipur University and Dr. Jiten Nongthombam of Centre of Myanmar Studies, Manipur University for making many sources of information available to me in the preparation of these lectures.

I am grateful to the Librarian, Mr. Prem Chand of the Institute and his staff for the assistance given to me. I also acknowledge the help of Mr. Sashank Thakur of Goa Civil Service who was formerly Academic Resource Officer and Mr. A.K. Sharma, PRO and the present Academic Resource Officer in arranging my lectures. I thank my daughter, Dr. (Ms) Jenpuiru Kamei and my wife Mrs. Lanshailu for the assistance during my residence in Shimla and academic atmosphere provided to me. I thank my friend, Mr. M.P. Misra of the Akansha Publishing House, New Delhi for his kind publication of the Lectures in a short notice.

Gangmumei Kamei

National Fellow IIAS

Shimla

25th November, 2011

1

Philosophy of History and the Historiography of Manipur

This lecture is a brief review of the epistemology of history and historiography. The history, historical knowledge, the philosophy of history, historical conscience, the mode of rational analysis or the scientific method constitute what is popularly known as the historical method. The basic tenets of historical method are the definition of history, nature and objective of historical studies, discovery of the historical facts, the reconstruction of the historical past, conceptualization, interpretation, generalization and periodization of the historical events.

The study of history has gone through many ages and stages. Regarding the definition of what is history, it was started with the classical historians of the ancient Greece. The term "History" originated from the Greek word, "*historia*" whose literal meaning was "inquiry". The great pioneer historians were Herodotus and Thucydides. Herodotus who wrote *Histories* [1] was regarded as the father of history and Thucydides, the author of the great classic, *History of the Polopennesian War* was another historian.[2] The Graeco-Roman historians more or less adopted the Greek method of writing history based on the available sources of information. Such Greek historians were described as "original historians" by Hegel, the great philosopher of history in his *Lectures on the Philosophy of World History* (1822-1830).[3] The original historians were the participant recorders of the historical events. The Graeco-Roman historiography was universally accepted in ancient Europe.

Whether the term "History" was equivalent with Sanskrit, *Itihas-Purana* was debated among the ancient Indian historians. Many scholars thought that *Itihas-Purana* would mean history. An etymological analysis of the two terms gives us a clear picture. According to the great Sanskrit lexicographer, V.S. Apte[4], the word "History" means "*Itihas*." *Itihas* meaning what it was or what had happened. Regarding "*Purana*", it has been described as "the Sacred and mythological poem" derived from Hindu religious myth and belief. *Purana* cannot cover History.[5] *Itihas* is more appropriate word for history. Romila Thapar thinks that Itihas Purana is a connotative word for history in Indian context as myth and tradition constitute a part of history. She writes,

> "The *Itihasa-Purana* is referred to in the *Arthasastra*. Its literal meaning is 'thus it was'. The events of the past were so related as to link this with the goals and purposes of tradition which was being historicized.[6]"

Another Sanskrit word *Vansavali* meaning the genealogy of the ruling families of principalities or kingdom is also widely used.

Christian Theological Historiography: St. Augustine: History as a Divine Plan

What is the purpose of History? The Christian theological historiography of Europe strongly emphasizes that the purpose of history which proceeds according to the divine plan is the ultimate realization of the eternal will of God for spiritual redemption of man or punishment of man in the hands of God. Christian historiography of the Middle Ages represented by St. Augustine was a type of historical determinism. St. Augustine (354-430) was the greatest thinker of the Christian political philosophy and Christian historiography of the medieval age. It is said that medievalism began with St. Augustine. Christianity had destroyed paganism. Roman Empire had accepted Christianity as its official religion. And Christianity had given a religious unity to the Europe and Roman Empire. St. Augustine lived in an extremely critical period for Rome and Christianity because of the Barbarian attacks on Rome. Their leaders, Alaric and Visigoths sacked Rome in A.D. 410. The destruction of the city of Rome and many things which the Roman civilization stood for appeared to be complete. There was a big debate, why the city of Rome was destroyed? Why did the Roman Empire decline? Many non-Christian leaders and writers attributed the fall of Rome to the acceptance of Christianity by the Roman Empire. Rome under the protection of her ancient gods had grown up from a mere city state to a world wide empire. Rome threw away its ancient religion and Christianity had brought ruin to Rome. Many lamented that Christianity could not save Rome from destruction. The criticism of this kind provoked St. Augustine to take up the defence of Christianity. And he wrote his famous classic, *De Civitate Dei* (The City of God) in 22 volumes between A.D 413 and A.D 426. The first 10 volumes were devoted to the defence of Christianity and the remaining 12 volumes to the explanation of the City of God.

The Eternal Will of God

St. Augustine developed the concept of the Eternal will of God to explain the historical development of the world. The fall of Rome was the part of the divine plan to create a new city of God on earth. According to St. Augustine, God had ordained order, regularity and beauty in nature. And the story of mankind depends not upon chance but upon the eternal will of the creator. There is divine will behind everything. The history of mankind was struggle between the forces of evil and forces of good. The forces of the evil were represented by the secular empires. But they were non- permanent and they must give place to the city or kingdom of God. Thus, St. Augustine and following him the Christian thinkers adopted a purely theologically approach to history writing. They composed a universal history based on chronology of the Old Testament and New Testament. They adopted a single chronological frame, based on the birth of Jesus Christ as the historical anchor period before Christ and after Christ. A prominent place was given to the idea of providence in the evolution of human history which was predestined to be redeemed or punished by Eternal will of God. The Christian historiography dominated the European historiography till the coming of the historiography of the Rationalist school of the 18th century. This is a classic example of the historical determinism in historiography. God as the creator of the universe and maker of empires and nations was accepted in the Oriental countries. The Graeco-Roman historiography was abandoned by the Christian theological historiography which adopted the theological method to explain and predict the ultimate victory of Christianity. As noted above, there are inadequacies of historical determinism in the ideas of St. Augustine. There is no philosophy of history in the writings of St. Augustine, only Christian theology. However, among the Arabs, their historiography was scientific and quite modern. We may refer to Ibn Khaldun, an Arab historian of Tunis who wrote the *Introduction of History* in 1377. Ibn Khaldun refers to the cultural, geographical and ecological factors in the evolution of history of the Arab world. Theological historiography of Europe was not acceptable to them. The modern concept of purpose of history is provided by E.H. Carr when he writes:

> "The function of the historian is neither to love the past nor to emancipate himself from the past but to master and understand it as the key to the understanding of the present. Great history is written purely when the historian's vision of the past is illuminated by the insight into the problem of the present. . . . The function of history is to promote a profounder understanding of both the past and the present through the interrelation between them."[7]

The Philosophy of History

Is there a philosophy of History? The term, "Philosophy of History" was first coined by the famous Enlightenment philosopher of France, Voltaire[8] who is regarded as the best representative of the Age of Reason and the rationalist resurrection against the orthodox theological Christian historiography in the middle ages. To Voltaire, "Philosophy of History" meant the idea of a critical and scientific history as distinct or differentiated from the Christian theological interpretation of history which was current in Europe since the Middle Ages. It requires a philosopher of Voltaire's scholarship, repute and influence to stand up against the Christian historiography with its strong belief in the divine providence as the motive force of history. Voltaire was a versatile writer whose views were highly respected by his contemporaries.

It was Hegel who developed his concept of philosophy of history in his famous *Lectures on the Philosophy of World History* (1822-30). Hegel was a great philosopher and he studied many histories of different countries. Hegel in his lecture of 1830 on the "Philosophical history of world" said: "The philosophy of history is nothing more than the application of thought to history". He divided history into three modes i.e. (a) original history, (b) reflective history and (c) the philosophical history.

Hegel was the foremost philosopher of the early nineteenth century and his views were accepted in the philosophical world of the western Europe. His philosophy of history was a part of his philosophical system to him, the idea or reason is the motive force of universal history or cosmic change. It develops in a dialectical process according to which one idea or proposition which he calls thesis is posed against another proposition which produces an anti thesis, out of which emerges a proposition which is common to both the opposing propositions in the form of a synthesis. And Hegel's philosophy of history is taken as thinking about the world as whole. It is also a critical and scientific appreciation of the process of change. Hegel raised the speculation on history as a distinct branch of philosophy.

Auguste Comte of France who founded the Positivist School of thought gave great importance to the study of history in the Europe. The Positivists tried to discover the uniform laws governing the societies and the social activities of men. And they added a dimension to the philosophy of history and made it a branch of social science. History is turning towards the social science.

Leopold Von Ranke and Empiricism

Hegel's philosophy of history gained a great respectability in the philosophical world. At the same time in Germany a very scientific and critical school of history based on empiricism was developed by the great historian, Leopold Von Ranke (1795-1886). Ranke and his school of historians dominated the history writing in Europe. Ranke followed and developed a historical methodology adopted by a German scholar Reinhold Neibuhr. The critical technique developed through sheer industry and intensive research, a new and more refined historical methodology was created. Ranke performed a yeoman's service to historical science which just entitled him as the founder of modern discipline of history. He tried to divorce the study of the past from the passion of the present. He insisted that the strict presentation of facts is the supreme law of historical writings. He also played a significant role in the teaching of history at the university level through the seminars at the University of Berlin. He published the first historical journal, *Historische Zaischrift* containing the true method of historical research. Ranke also developed the science of the evidence of historiography. He was the greatest historian of the nineteenth century.

Hegelian philosophy and dialectics were applied by Karl Marx in his *Communist Manifesto*, (1848) in the economic interpretation in the evolution of human civilization from primitive communism to slave based empire to feudalism to capitalism and ultimately communism. Through Marx's writings, particularly, economic interpretation of history has become an important tool of Marxian philosophy. However, with the growth of empirical data made available by empirical historians, the philosophy of history was overwhelmed by the empiricism of Ranke and his followers.

Eminent historians with the original knowledge of historical methodology started a scientific study at the universal and at the national level. In the eighteenth century, Gambattista Vico (1688-1744) adopted the scientific method. Vico contributed to the scientific methodology in history writing. Lord Acton in Britain, Beniditto Croce in Italy (*History as a story of Liberty*), Oswald

Spongler (*The decline of the West*) were the great historians. Three philosophers of History may be noted, R.G. Collingwood (*The Ideas of History*, 1945), Marc Bloch (*The Historian's Craft*, 1946) and E.H. Carr (*What is history?*, 1962). The philosophy of History and the Historical Method are well integrated in the writings of these historian-philosophers.

We may quote the remarkable statements of R.G. Collingwood, Marc Bloch and E.H. Carr.

R.G. Collingwood observes:

> "All history is history of thought and therefore all history is reenactment in the historians thought whose history he is studying" (R.G. Collingwood, *Ideas of History* p. 215: 1945).

History is a re-enactment of the past experience thought through the mind of the historian. Collingwood's view of history is more concerned with the mode of reasoning or the thinking of the historian on the past. It is more a philosophical inquiry of the past. The reenactment or reconstruction of the past in the historian's mind is dependent on the empirical evidence. History is to be located in time and space. The historian's evidence necessitates that history has to deal with the facts of the past which are reenacted in the mind of the historian.

Marc Bloch's *The Historian's Craft* has made history purely a scientific work. He made the historical reasoning as the philosophy of history. He raised history to a stage of science. He said:

> "We have called history the science of man".

He continues,

> "This is still far too vague. It is necessary to add of men in time".

History is a science of man in time.

E.H. Carr thinks that:

> "History is a continuous process of interaction between the historian and his facts, an unending dialogue between the present and past."

According to Carr, history is also a study of the causes of the facts of the past and interpreting them. Collingwood is more abstract and philosophical while Carr is more empirical and interpretative as they represent the two trends in the historiography of modern times. These two thinkers have raised the study of history to a higher philosophic level.

It is in this context that history is now not only a true account of what really happened in the past, how and why of the past happenings. History means more an approach, a mode of inquiry to find the truth and interpret the truth to the relevance of the present. It has become more a question of method. Hence, our concern with the historical method. How the historian reenacts the past in his mind, and how the historian conducts his interaction with his facts of historical evidence and how he carries on the dialogue between the past and present, how the interpretation of the past facts is done, what is the role of reason or reasoning, historical thinking or reasoning facts or historical evidence, these are the issues of historical method.

Thus, the philosophy of history has been concerned with the investigation and discovery of the past, meaning and interpretation of the historical phenomena, speculation about the nature and use of history. What will be the procedure of the historical thinking or reasoning has to be located in the method which has come popularly as the historical method.

The Historical Method

In short, Historical Method is the answer to the question 'what is history?. The historical method has assumed a great importance with the development of the scientific history. After a long debate, history has been put rightfully in the category of science, or to be precise of social science. Science is both an accumulator of knowledge and a method of approach in the search of the truth and knowledge. It is also a rational mode of analysis to arrive at and find out the truth. History, being a mode of rational inquiry is science and real history is a scientific history. And history adopts a scientific method which means a rational and logical mode of inquiry, analysis and generalization. The historical method is a tool to answer the question of history, like what happens, how it happens and why it happens.

Historical method is the mode of historical reasoning adopted by the historian. It covers the following phases and process.

(i) The location and selection of the historical facts, evidence of process relevant to the objective of the historical investigation.

(ii) Construction or reconstruction of the past based on the analysis of the facts and evidences.

(iii) Interpretation of the historical facts.

This method is more or less explained by Marc Bloch in his *The Historian's Craft*.

The Historical Evidence

Primacy of facts in the historical study has been well-established. Historical enquiry starts with the location and selection of facts which are essential for the construction of a phenomenon of history. All facts are not necessarily historical evidence; it is relative to the objective, theme and manner of the historical evidence has been now called the source of history.

Historical Observation

In the location and identification of facts, the mode of historical observation is applied. Here the scientific observation which is carried out directly by the scientist who is working with hypotheses. In the case of historical observation, it is not possible for a historian to observe the happenings which constitute history. His observation is an indirect one, following on the facts or observation. He is of course, required to have a wide knowledge of human activists, past and present. Peculiarity of historical observation is that it has to observe the events through document by reading or examining the evidences for a historical reconstruction.

Authenticity of the Evidence

Once a fact has been located and identified as historical evidence, the authenticity of the particular evidence is scrutinized, tested and finally proved. There are many instances in which book, chronicles, inscriptions and other historical evidences are forged. The crucial test of the reasoning faculty of the historian is on the establishment of the historical evidence.

The principle of historical criticism, according to Marc Bloch requires the asking of the questions as given below:

(i) Are the evidence forged or deceptive?

(ii) Do the evidences speak the truth?

(iii) How are the evidences to be subjected to scientific and rational scrutiny?

After the establishment of the authenticity of the evidences the historian, after close observation and scrutiny, will assemble the documents which may be literary and archaeological. He can criticize, reject or accept the evidence based on his findings.

Selection of Evidences

It is the prerogative of the historian to select the evidences needed for his construction of the history of his field of study. But a practising historian, following the historical method, he cannot indulge in the irrational and irrelevant evidences. Otherwise, his work will lack, the rationally, consistency and relevance.

Reconstruction of the Past

The facts, thus, selected, will be subjected to the historical analysis and utilized for the reconstruction of the past. In this process of historical analysis, the historical impartiality is to be rigorously applied for an objective judgement and understanding of the phenomenon of history. It calls for rational organization of the facts which Marc Bloch calls the raw materials of history.

However, different schools of history writing have adopted different approaches in the construction of the past. For the determinist school of thought such as the Marxian's, the evidences of economic problem are utilized for the writing of history based on the economic determinism. This is greatly linked up with another question of interpretation. Reconstruction and interpretation are dependent on the model of history writing which is adopted in a particular case. However, the historian's supreme duty is to explain the cause of the happenings in the past in this construction.

Interpretation of the Past

The real testing of the historical method is on the question of interpretation. Sometimes the historical method and the mode of historical interpretation are almost taken as one method. Whether a history is a critical history or traditional history or scissors and patch history (of Collingwood) or scientific history or determinist history, it is dependent on the category of historical interpretation. The usual issues of the objectivity and generalization in history are engrained in this interpretation of the past.

The scholars of different disciplines, ranging from the Enlightenment, the philosophers and political thinkers had interpreted history in different way. One school known as "Historicism" has grown up to explain that every aspect of literature, culture, philosophical thought can be explained by history. Historicism was meant for the explanation and interpretation of history in relation to specific issues. Historicism is a wide field of historical interpretation. It is not proposed to deal with Historicism but it has become a wide field of study.

Historical Objectivity

Objectivity in history, in a negative sense, is not taking side by the historian in the interpretation of history. The historian is both rational and passionate. Based on reason and historical reasoning, the historian is expected to produce a rational and objective history. But the subjectivity is an outcome of human passion and the historian is likely, very often to fall a prey to this subjective pressure. The colonial or imperial historiographer defends the imperial actions while the nationalist historian eulogizes the patriotic acts and condemns the imperial authorities. A scientific historian is supposed to give an objective history. How the objectivity is to be established? For example, when a fact passes through the historian's mind, the fact is coloured by his own prejudices and bias in his mind. The fact is likely to be biased. When the fact is constructed into a historical canvass, the choice of the fact is not objective but has become subjective. Objectivity demands that when the fact passes through the historian's mind, his judgement should be free from prejudices and biases. While objectivity is definitely an ideal in historical method; total objectivity cannot be fully achieved. This is due to the very nature of history which is as somebody said, not an exact science. We may refer to Ranke who is of the opinion that once the facts are subjected to criticism and cured of their dross by the historian's craftsmanship, the fact becomes pure and unalloyed historical gold.

Generalization

It was Auguste Comte, of the Positivist school who tried to locate the uniform laws and of the empirical historical data to explain the growth of the structure of the society. The historian applies the principle of generalization to find the uniformity in the historical date to discover the universal laws. Historical generalization means that after the analysis of the historical data, an abstraction is deduced to show certain common pattern or patterns in the historical development. The process of abstraction may be called generalization. As history is now a social science, out of the historical data, generalized patterns of history emerges through the abstraction. The abstraction of the historical data is the generalization of history

Periodization

History deals with time and space; so, chronology and geography are important parts of a historical inquiry with the new approach to history. The study of human history in term of period has been increasingly discarded and study of specific problem of history, in the word of Lord Acton has become fashionable. Marx's economic interpretation of history in the evolution of human civilization from primitive communism, slave based empire, to feudalism, capitalism and to communism has almost destroyed the chronological history. But so long, history has to deal with the past of man, it is concerned with time and "Periodization" in history continues to exist in the historical method.

It is not proposed to discuss in this lecture the Marxian historiography which is a great field of historical studies. We will neither deal with the Anallist School of Historiography of France nor with the subaltern school or history from below of Indian historiography.

Different schools of historiography grew up in different countries. Of these, Marxian historiography developed by Karl Marx and his followers forms a distinctive method of history writing universally. The Annalist School of France which was based on solid empirical foundation is important school of Europe. In India there grew up a group of brilliant historians who founded the school of subaltern history or history from below. This had become a very popular school of historiography adopted in almost all countries. The periodization of history was adopted on the basis of theme. So schools like the post-colonial historiography and ethnic historiography have come up. A survey of these schools of history writing cannot be covered by the present paper.

Historiography of Manipur

Manipur was an ancient kingdom with a long history and rich culture. Manipur means the land or city of the gems. It was named so in the early eighteenth century (1724) by the Hinduised king Garibniwaz (1709-1748). The pre-Hindu names of the kingdom were Poireipak, Meitrabak and Kangleipak. The dominant communities are the Meiteis who live in Manipur valley; the others are the hill tribes, the Nagas and the Kuki-Chins who dwell in the surrounding hills.

Manipur valley is a cradle of human civilization and culture. Different ethnic groups migrated to Manipur in search of land, resources, fame and glory. The Meitei kingdom grew up in the Manipur valley while in the hills, the tribals did not build up polity formation beyond the village polity.

The ancient Meiteis developed the knowledge of writing quite early. They possess strong sense of history and as we are all aware, historiography is the art of writing history. The historiography of Manipur may be divided into the following categories:

1. Traditional Meitei historiography.
2. Colonial historiography.
3. Post-colonial historiography and
4. Tribal historiography.

In terms of periodization these categories cover three periods of history of Manipur; pre-colonial, colonial and Post-colonial.

The Traditional Meitei Historiography

The traditional concept of history is expressed by the Meitei word *"Puwari"* (the story of fore-fathers). This term is nearer to the Sanskrit *"Itihas"* rather than the English "History" or Greek "*Historia.*" The Meitei *Puwari* consists of the myths, legends and historical accounts of their country. The creation myths or cosmological traditions, origin and genealogies of the clans, the religious accounts, the dynastic accounts of the clan chieftains are given prominent place. We may refer to another word "*Puya*" which is like the Sanskrit *Purana*. *Puya* is a historical text which records the myths, genealogy, historical tradition etc. Chronicles with or without chronology formed the core of Meitei historical literature. However, history as a separate academic discipline did not exist. It was a part of the whole gamut of knowledge. For example, a literary text of the eighteenth century, *Leithak Leikharol* which is a compendium of myths, legends, genealogy, folklore, religious practice and social accounts, is not a history in the modern sense, but a standard book of knowledge which is expected to be possessed by a traditional Meitei scholar known as the Maichou.

In the early stage of Meitei civilization the record keeping or chronicle keeping was started. There were literary texts dealing with historical events since the beginning of Christian era as claimed by ancient writers. Education and scholarship were controlled by the royalty and nobility. This had led to the monopoly of knowledge by a very few scholars patronized and utilized by the monarch. The king-controlled writing was reflected in the chronicle keeping. The Meitei view of the past was a holistic approach. Naturally it was difficult to separate what was historical from what were myth, legend, tradition, religion and theology.

History writing was dominated by the interest or consideration of the royalty and priestly class. There was no separate discipline of history as such. History or historical knowledge was part of the whole knowledge. As mentioned above, a Meitei Maichou was a scholar, a priest, an astrologer and an advisor to the royalty or nobility. Practical necessity required the Maichous to look at society, state and religion as a whole. And the knowledge of the Maichou became a generalized and comprehensive one or with some great scholar encyclopedic. Historical particularism or special differentiation of history did not develop in the ancient period.

Chronicles and *puyas* were not only the "historical pieces" but they were used as manuals of administration, religious rites, social and judicial dispensation and cultural affairs. Perhaps, it was due to this reason that history as a distinct and separate branch of knowledge did not develop in ancient Manipur. And the objective of history of the ancient Meitei was to know the past, use the knowledge of the past for the present needs; and the action and achievement of the past should be kept for the knowledge of posterity. The king and nobility had a strong concern for the posterity. They tried to preserve what was achieved by the monarch in the past for perpetuation of their fame. The idea of the past was greatly influenced by the need of the present and by a desire for glorification by the posterity. Hence, the great concern for control over event recording chronicles. The greatest chronicle of this type is the royal chronicle known as the "*Cheitharol Kumbaba.*"

With the sanskritization of Manipur, deliberate attempt was made by the Hindu scholars to imprint an Aryan and Hindu origin and identity on the Hinduised Meitei. The identification of religion and race had led to the emergence of a distinct sense of origin and a view of history on the part of the ruling dynasty. History was given a sanskritized orientation which was reflected in the chronicles and genealogy of the ruling Ningthouja dynasty of Manipur. The keeping of chronicles which was an indigenous Meitei practice was given a chronological frame by the adoption of Hindu calendars; for instance the celebrated Cheitharol Kumbaba, the royal chronicle of Manipur adopted three eras, *Kalyabda*, *Sakabda* and *Chandrabda*. The Ningthourol *Kumbaba* and other genealogical chronicles do not have chronology. The absence of time frame of chronology is a reflection of the Meitei concept of past which intermingles with the present. The past and the present exist side by side in the Meitei psyche. Since, there was no technology of printing before the British rule the chronicles or historical texts were not printed or published but kept in the Pandit Loishang (royal college of priest). The *Cheitharol Kumbaba* was an official diary; the royalty's view and version were recorded.

We give below a few historical texts which may be described as the part of the traditional Meitei historiography.

Historical Chronicles

They are the royal chronicles, especially the *Cheitharol Kumbaba*, *Ningthourol Kumbaba*, a royal chronicle without chronology which gives more detail than the *Cheitharol Kumbaba*. They have been already published.

1. *Kangbalon: The Genealogy of Kangba*, the first ruler of the Meiteis in the proto-historical period.
2. *Pakhangba Phamban,* The coronation of Pakhangba, the founder of the Ningthouja dynasty of the first century A.D.
3. *Pakhangba Nongkarol* (death of Pakhangba)
4. *Poireiton Khunthokpa*, the immigration of Poireiton, a colonizer in Manipur Valley in the first century A.D.
5. *Naothingkhong Phamban*, coronation of Naothingkhong of the eighth century.
6. *Loyamba Shilyen*, the administrative decree of King Loyamba (A.D.1094-1122). It is regarded as the first written constitution of Manipur. The decree was issued on A.D. 1110.
7. *Pong Meitei Lamyen Lairik*, Treaty on demarcation of boundary between Mau Shan kingdom of Pong, Upper Burma and Meiteis in the year 1471.
8. *Thiren Layat*, an account of the religious belief of the Meitei written in the reign of the King Khagemba (1597-1652). No name of the author.
9. *Ava Ngamba* (war against Burma written by Nungambam Govindaram). It was an account of Manipur war against Burma during the reign of Garibniwaz.
10. *Takhel Ngamba* (an account of the war against Tripura written by Govindaram).
11. *Khahi Ngamba* (conquest of Khasi by Maharaja Ghambir Singh in 1829).
12. *Telainlanda Nara Singh* (King Nara Singh in the battle of Telain; Nara Singh's role in the battle of Telian against the Burmese during the 1st Anglo-Burmese war).
13. *Zilla Darbar*, The durbar between Maharaja Chandrakriti Singh and Lord Northbrooke, Viceroy of India at Silchar on the Barak river in 1872.

The following works were written by Manipuri scholars based on indigenous historical sources of information

1. Haodeijamba Chaitnya, *Manipur Itihas 1890*, published in Sylhet, Bengal. It was a first book on history of Manipur published before British conquest of Manipur and printed in Bengali script.
2. The second one was *Manipur Purabrita* which was written by Pukhrambam Parijat and published in 1917. It was published with the permission of Raja Churachand Singh of Manipur. It was supposed to be a reply to T.C. Hodson's book 'The Meitheis' regarding ethnic and linguistic identity of the Meiteis.
3. The next work was *Manipur Itti britti* written by Khumanthem Kaomacha Singh (1938).
4. Another one was *Bijoy Panchali* by Mutum Jhulon Singh.
5. Panditraj Atombapu Sharma, the great scholar of Manipur wrote *Manipur Itihas* in 1940.

These works though written during the colonial period are traditional in style. So they are part of the traditional Meitei historiography.

Colonial Historiography

The British conquered Manipur in 1891; and the colonial era in the history of Manipur was started but Manipur had more than a century of relation with the British since 1762. The first trade treaty between the East India Company and Raja Jai Singh (Bhagyachandra Singh) was signed in that year. But the treaty failed. The deep engagement between the British and Manipur was carried out during the first Anglo-Burmese War (1824-1826). The Burmese conquered Assam, Manipur, Jaintia and Cachar and the Burmese force posed a great threat to the British Province of Bengal. Manipur wanted the British help to drive away the Burmese from Manipur. At the same time the British wanted allies among the fugitive princes of Manipur to drive away the Burmese from Assam, Jaintia and Cachar. There was a convergence of interest between the British and Manipur. By an alliance between David Scott, the Agent of the Governor General and Raja Gambhir Singh of Manipur, the Manipur Levy of five hundred soldiers recruited by Gambhir Singh in 1824 drove out the Burmese out of Manipur beyond the Kabaw Valley. By the treaty of Yandabo (1826) which concluded the Anglo-Burmese War, Burmese were driven out of whole northeast India. British conquered Assam, Jaintia and Cachar. The Treaty of Yandabo recognized Raja Gambhir Singh as an independent King of Manipur. Manipur was liberated and the country was reconstructed. A close Anglo-Manipur relationship was developed.

The British officers who participated in the Anglo-Burmese War and who helped Manipur in the reconstruction of the country were capable officers. Most of them were not only bold soldiers and capable administrative officers; they were great writers who left behind excellent reports on geography, history, culture and many ethnological accounts for the benefit of the posterity. The names of David Scott, the first Commissioner of Assam, Francis Jenkins, another commissioner, R.B. Pemberton, F.J. Grant who helped the Manipur Levy of Gambhir Singh, and participated in the negotiation with the Burmese over Kabaw Valley are still remembered.

For the whole northeast India, we have the excellent account of R.B. Pemberton, the *Report on the northeast frontier of British India* published in 1835. This report devoted a sizeable portion on Manipur history, geography, economy and ethnography. R.B. Pemberton as a young officer volunteered to accompany Gambhir Singh in the liberation of Manipur. He was a pioneer of modern historical studies. Pemberton's report was based on the style of James Mill's *History of India* published in the year 1819 which was the first history of India in English language. Pemberton's report is still relevant to the states and peoples of north east frontier and Upper Burma.

There were official reports and accounts published by British officers posted as Political Agents in Manipur. Mention may be made of Major W. McCulloch's *Account of the Valley of Munnipore and surrounding Tribes* published in 1859 at Calcutta. McCulloch was in Manipur for nearly 23 years from 1844-1867. He was engaged by Maharaja Nara Singh in the settlement of the Kuki influx in Manipur. He married a Manipuri princess and helped Nara Singh and his successors particularly Maharaja Chandrakriti Singh for political stability in Manipur. Later on he settled in Shillong and died in 1885. McCulloch's account is a brief report but it is mostly authentic and reliable. His account deals with early history of Manipur particularly 18th century and first half of 19th century. His knowledge of the hill tribe was quite profound. He classified the tribes of Manipur as Nagas and Kukis. His description of Meitei society is even now relevant. He also studied languages of the tribes and communities of Manipur. So the ethnographic account of the tribes and communities is helpful for the reconstruction of the social history of Manipur.

Another Political Agent, Dr. R. Brown, a surgeon by profession, wrote *A Statistical Account of Manipur* and it was published in 1874. It was perhaps modelled after a guideline given by Sir W.W. Hunter, the Director General of Statistics, Government of India. Sir W.W. Hunter was the editor of two volumes to *Account of Assam*. Brown's *Statistical Account* was written after the gazetteer type. Brown's account includes geography, history, religion, social account and ethnography. Though it is not history, it contains valuable historical information.

After Brown's *Statistical Account*, there was the *Gazetteer of Manipur* compiled and published by Captain E.W. Dun in 1886 (an abridged edition was published in 1891). Captain Dun was an intelligence officer. His gazetteer was published as a secret document from Shimla. Dun's account deals with the history of Manipur since the Anglo-Burmese War. He also gives a narrative of Anglo-Manipur relation. He declares that Manipur was an independent kingdom. He describes the politics in Manipur, the monarchy, the nobility and the army. Dun's original document with authentic maps is an extremely important work for the reconstruction of the history of Manipur. A great landmark in the history of colonial historiography of north east India occurred in 1884 when *A History of the relations of the hill tribes with the Government of British Bengal* was published by Alexander Mackenzie. Mackenzie was a competent member of the Indian Civil Service in the Government of Bengal. He had in 1869 published a highly documented report known as the Memorandum of the North Eastern Frontier. This report was highly praised by the Foreign Department of the Government of India. There was a pressure on him to publish a new edition of this memorandum. But Mackenzie who was the Home Secretary of the Government of Bengal who had access to the document and correspondence both in the home, judicial, revenue and foreign proceedings decided to make a review of British Government policies towards the hill tribes of the north east India. A group of hill tribes of eastern Himalayas to the north bank of the Brahmaputra were completely reviewed. Another group of tribes mostly the Nagas of the Patkoi hills, Sibsagar areas and southern Naga Hills was covered. The tribes of Khasi and Jaintia Hills, Lushai hills and Chittagong hill tracts were covered. With regard to Manipur, Mackenzie wrote that Manipur was an independent State; therefore Manipur state was outside the scope of his book. However, Manipur was a protected State and Manipur occupied a special place in the politics of northeast India.

Many scholars had praised Mackenzie's work as a great work of the colonial historiography. He was a great chronicler of events dealt by the then British Government with full facts at his command and with great responsibility in deciding policy affairs. He had written very nicely. His book has been praised as a great ethno history of the hill tribes. No student of history can ignore his work. Mackenzie as an analyst of historical events of the hill tribes of north east perhaps could not do justice. It was beyond the preview of his work.

Another semi-historical account based on personal experiences dealing with expansion of the British Political Agency and administration was *My Experience in Manipur and Naga Hills* written by Sir James Johnstone published posthumously in 1896 in London. Sir James Johnstone (1841-1896) was a Political Agent of Manipur. He served in the Keonjar district of Orissa. He acted as a Political Officer in the newly established Naga Hills district. James Johnstone's book makes a pleasant reading full of facts dealing with military operation, diplomatic relation, administrative affairs and keeping boundary affairs with Burma in peace. This book is not history but contains a lot of historical information. His views on men and affairs of Manipur are of great interest. He had a great vision for Manipur. Though it is semi historical it can be grouped under the source of history.

After the British conquest of Manipur British officers wrote on Manipur. B.C. Allen's, *The Gazetteer of Naga Hills and Manipur* (1905) makes a useful and informative reading on history, geography, society and culture of Manipur.

Last of the works on the colonial historiography was a *History of the Areas Bordering Assam*. It was written by Sir Robert Reid, a Governor of Assam in 1942. Reid's book is supposed to be continuation of Mackenzie's history ending in 1884. Like Mackenzie, Reid had access to all the official documents. He divided the history by political units. Manipur state constitutes a chapter of the history. Unfortunately, Reid's book is a compilation of documents. The author was not a historian. He was a mere documenter. His work lacks a central theme. This is not a history. However, for Manipur and other areas the information is very important. This book contains the historical narratives of Anglo-Manipur war of 1891, the execution of Chief Commissioner of Assam and his officers, and ultimate conquest of Manipur. It deals with the anti-British colonial movement such the Kuki Rebellion (1917-1919), the movement of Jadonang and Gaidinliu (1930-1933), the Women Agitation of Manipur Valley (1939-40). The narrative ended in 1940.

T.C. Hodson's *The Meitheis* (1908) was a classic anthropological study on the Meiteis. This is the best work on the Meiteis in the twentieth century. Hodson was the great writer with the knowledge of anthropology. This work made the Meiteis known in the English speaking anthropological world. Hodson supplemented his study with his knowledge of Meitei linguistic Hudson clearly shows on the ethnological and linguistic ground that the Meiteis are Tibeto-Burman. Abdul Ali was the first Indian historian to write on Manipur. His Notes on early history of Manipur deals with the early contact of Manipur with East India Company and subsequent relation between the two.

An important work of the colonial period is the *History of Assam Rifles* written by L.W. Shakespeare and published in 1929. This history traces the glorious exploits of this famous Assam Rifles which was born out of a para military force known as the Cachar Levy of 1835. This history deals with the Anglo-Manipur conflict of 1891 and the suppression of Kuki Rebellion (1917-1919) which are an important aspect of colonial history of Manipur.

The colonial historiography is not enormous and it does not contain much of history. The colonial writers did not deal with the central theme of history of Manipur. Subsequent writers of the post independence historiography or post-colonial period are supplied with the information whatever sketchy it may be in the reconstruction of history of the north east region including the state of Manipur.

The Meitei polity, society, religion, culture and folklore had been fully studied. The racial and ethnic identity was again raised. The colonial writers did not accept the Aryan origin of the Hinduised Meitei.

During the colonial period, the study of archeology was begun. W. Yumjao Singh was the pioneer archeologist of Manipur. *The Report on Archeological Studies,* Vol. I, 1935 was a comprehensive report on inscriptions, historical monuments and numismatics. Yumjao Singh discovered the Phayeng Copper Plates of King

Khongtekcha. He gave critical comments on the royal chronicle of Manipur known as the *Cheitharol Kumbaba*.

An issue which was raised by the Brahmanical scholars was their effort to refute the alleged statement by N.N. Vasu in Bengali encyclopaedia, *Viswakosh* that the Hindu Meiteis were non-Aryan and Mongoloid. The debate was carried over in post-Independence period. The pioneer of the school was the great Pandit Raj Atombapu Sharma.

Historiography of the Second World War in Manipur has been studied by the British army officers, the leaders of Indian National Army and followers of Netaji Subhas Chandra Bose and by the military officers of the Japanese Army. While Field Marshal William Slim's book *Defeat into Victory* was a overview of the exploits of British 14th Army, the work of George Evans and Anthony Brett-James, *Imphal: A Flower on Lofty Heights*, *The Springing Tiger* by Hugh Toy gave the military history of the Japanese invasion, S.C. Bose's *The History of the Indian National Army* is an important account of the war.

The Post-colonial Historiography

The contemporary historiography was started after British departure from Manipur. However, the post independence period may be taken as the beginning of post colonial period in historiography. Post-colonialism is initially an approach of English language literature in those countries which were under the British colonial rule. A huge literature on post-colonial theme was produced by both persons of literature, sociology, political science and now by the scholars of history. It was a reaction to things colonial from the scholars of post-colonial times. We may now locate post-colonial in the historiography of Manipur. Manipur has had a colonial experience. The colonial historiography was incomplete and did not have a balanced view of the people and their history. They created a hiatus between the inhabitants on religious consideration, Hindu Meitei and non-Hindu tribes. They projected themselves as the saviour of the tribes from the dominant

Meiteis. The colonial historiography refused to accept the Meitei traditional views on their origin, and history which were influenced by the Bhramanical scholars. They did not try to give any credence to the indigenous Meitei historiography.

However in the post-colonial period, an attempt was made by the historians to write a composite history of Manipur. There were two trends. One was the continuation of the writings of the Brahmanical school; the other was more or less a scientific historical school. The reassessment of history and historical events was carried out. The historian tried to glorify the history of the pre colonial and the colonial period. Under the post-colonial historiography, the hill tribes start demanding a place in the history and historiography of Manipur.

Between 1947 and 1991 four works on history of Manipur were published. R.K. Sanahal Singh published *Manipur Itihas* in Manipuri in 1947. It was a pioneering history with a scientific method based on chronicles of Manipur and British archival information and Bengali sources. This book is a contribution to post colonial historiography. The second one was J. Roy's *History of Manipur* published in 1958. It was a first history of Manipur in English and widely circulated in India. The scope of his book was limited, starting from the 18th century only. The author did not have much access to the indigenous sources in Manipuri. The third one, R.K. Jhalajit Singh's *A short history of Manipur* published in 1965 was a comprehensive history based on royal chronicle of the Ningthouja dynasty. The history covers all the periods of history, ancient, medieval and modern from first century to the Merger of Manipur to the Indian Union (1949). He utilized the indigenous sources in Manipuri language and the British archival sources. His objective was to record the expansion of Aryan culture and Hinduism to Manipur. He was under the influence of Brahminical School of history writing that the Meiteis are ethnically and linguistically Indo-Aryan. Gangmumei Kamei's *History of Manipur Pre-Colonial Period* was published in 1991 in the last decade of the 20th century. This work is a well researched history.

It covers the ancient and medieval period. He based this history on the original sources. This is a widely circulated work. The author applied the scientific method of historiography in this book.

A category of writings dealing with specific aspects of history and polity were published between 1953 and 1970. They are Atombapu Sharma's *Pakhangba* (1953) dealing with religious history, Nandalal Sharma's *Meitrabak* (1960) dealing with ancient Manipuri literature, the political system of Manipur and last days of Independence of the State, N. Ibobi Singh's *Manipur Administration* (1966) which describes the political system of Manipur in the 18th and 19th centuries and *Manipur Itihas* (1970) written by L. Chandramani Singh dealing with Anglo-Manipur relation up to the 19th century. The books of N. Ibobi Singh and L. Chandramani Singh's were the works of their doctoral research.

Publication of Cheitharol Kumbaba, the royal chronicle (1967)

The pandits of Manipur who had connection with the Pandit Loishang of the royal court had examined the royal chronicles in ancient Meitei script. The manuscripts of the chronicle were kept in the royal college of priest (Pandit Loishang) but the common man scholars could not get access to it. Some attempts were made to publish this chronicle. Mention may be made of the abridged version of *Cheitharol Kumbaba* published by Pandit Thongam Madhab Singh in 1939. But it was L.M. Iboongohal Singh who was a Judge and member of the Manipur State Durbar during Maharaja Churachand Singh's rule took the initiative of collecting the manuscript from the court with the help of Maharaja himself. And this chronicle was written out in Bengali script with the help of some pandits and handed over the same to the Manipuri Sahitya Parishad. The chronicle was edited by L.M. Iboongohal Singh and Pandit N. Khelchandra Singh. For authenticity and public respectability, the Manipuri Sahitya Parishad, the apex body of Manipuri literature published *Cheitharol Kumbaba* in 1967. This publication was a great landmark in the historiography of Manipur.

Cheitharol Kumbaba is a compound of two words, combination of two practices of royal court. *Cheithaba* is a system of counting years of the Meitei Calendar under the lunar system. The year of the calendar was named after an individual who volunteered to be a scape goat of the evils of the king, country and people for a particular year. In return he was given a reward of one *pari* (hectare) of tax free land. He was called the *Cheithaba* of the year. The system of *Cheithaba* was started in A.D. 1484 during the reign of King Kyamba. All the names of the *Cheithaba* are even today recorded by Pandit Loishang. Kumbaba means counting of years (*kum* - year, *paba* - counting). So Cheitharol Kumbaba literally means counting of years according to the name of Cheithaba. The keeping of the chronicle was started from the 15th century. The chronicle gives a genealogy of kings of the Ningthouja dynasty from Nongdalairen Pakhangba to Bodhchandra Singh (A.D. 33 to 1955). The *Cheitharol Kumbaba* gives a list of 78 kings of Manipur. There were 37 kings of Manipur recorded before King Kyamba who started the chronicle keeping. So the reconstruction of the accounts of the chronicle before 1484 must have been carried out by the royal scholars and astrologers by collecting information from many other sources.

There have been many instances of rewriting the chronicle due to repeated foreign invasions particularly the Burmese and the British. There are many valid questions to be put on the recordings in the chronicles. Unless scrutinized properly the authenticity of the contents cannot be completely accepted. *The Cheitharol Kumbaba* edited by Pandit N. Khelchandra Singh has gone into several editions 1967, 1989 and 2009. A large number of chronicles mostly of the clans had been published since 1967.

In 1995, another version of *Cheitharol Kumbaba* was published with a new title *The Lost Kingdom*. This copy was translated from the original *Cheitharol Kumbaba* by Bamacharan Mukherjee who was a clerk in the British Political Agency. After British conquest in 1891, Bamacharan Mukherjee was commissioned to translate the chronicle into English. Mukherjee took the help of 14 pandits in collection of the different versions of *Cheitharol Kumbaba* and translating it to English. It took six years to complete the translation. L. Joychandra Singh, a journalist and a polo enthusiast discovered the copy of this Kumbaba in British Library and Record Office in London. He published *The Lost Kingdom* in 1995. The English version was very brief and different in details from Manipuri version.

Another version of the *Cheitharol Kumbaba* was published in 2005. It was entitled, *The Court Chronicle of the Kings of Manipur The Cheitharon Kumpapa*, translated by Saroj Nalini Arambam Parratt. Saroj Nalini Parratt was an anthropologist by training. She worked in Birmingham University along with her husband Professor John Parratt. She had already done research on religion, history and culture of Manipur. Manipuri was her mother tongue. She studied manuscripts of *Cheitharol Kumbaba* in the custody of several scholars of Manipur like Pandit Ngarianbam Kulachandra, Thongam Madhab, Nameirakpam Dinachandra, Kharaibam Deva, of course, the 1967 edition of *Cheitharol Kumbaba* published by Manipuri Sahitya Parishad. It was published by Routledge, Taylor and Francis Group, London. The second volume came out in 2009. Saroj Nalini Parratt's versions contain the chronicle in the Meitei script. She gives the English translation. It also contains the list of kings. The first volume covers the period A.D. 33 to A.D. 1763. The second volume covers the period 1764 to 1955. There is also glossary of Manipuri words which makes the reading of the archaic word easy. It was supplemented by the specimen of Government approved Meitei Mayek script. Saroj Nalini Arambam Parratt had done a yeoman service to the oriental historiography particularly historiography of Manipur by publishing this chronicle.

During the post-colonial period, there were a lot of interests in the history of Manipur which were an outcome of the several historical controversies. The first question which has been debated for more than 300 years was whether the present Manipur was the Manipur of the *Mahabharata*, secondly did the Pandava hero

Arjuna visit Manipur and married a Manipuri princess Chitragada and a son named Babrubahan was born of the union of Arjuna and Chitragada? The Brahmin priests and scholars of Brahma Sabha presided by the Maharaja strongly argued that Arjuna visited Manipur and the ruling dynasty was descended from the Pandava hero and the ruling family was of Aryan origin. This was not accepted by the British scholars during the colonial period. This issue came up during the post-colonial period. The scholars of the indigenous Meitei Sanamahi religion argued that present Manipur was not Manipur of the Mahabharata and there was no Aryan connection of Manipur. This view is gaining more support. There are a large numbers of scholars of the Sanamahi School who wrote both in English and Manipuri (Meitei-lon) on their version of history, origin and culture which are gaining popularity and respectability. We may mention the names of Kangjia Gopal, S. Nilbir and K.C. Tensuba.

Archeology, epigraphy and numismatics had made progress since the time of W. Yumjao Singh. The contributions of O.K. Singh, Matuwa Bahadur, L. Kunjeshwari, P. Gunindra, Gourachandra Singh, K. Sabita and S. Bheigya Singh to these fields are really great. The recent restoration of the Kangla Fort is well documented by Pandit N. Khelchandra Singh, Rupabon Singh and S. Bheigya Singh in the book, *Kangla, ancient capital of Manipur,* 2008.

Another historical issue was concerned with the Anglo-Manipur war of 1891 particularly the battle of Khongjom. After conquest of Manipur by British in 1891, the British did not encourage any glorification of the princes of Manipur who were either executed or sentenced to life imprisonment. The conqueror did not like the conquered's sacrifices to be known to the people. But a Manipuri soldier who participated in the battle of Khongjom composed a ballad comprising every stage and style of fighting between the British soldiers and the Manipuri soldiers. True, the battle of Khongjom marked the end of the war and independence of Manipur. So this ballad known as Khongjom parva was sung throughout the country. The ballad replaces the history. After independence and after the Merger of Manipur into India, historians, intellectuals, political leaders, common men started a fresh look at the Anglo-Manipur war particularly the heroes, Jubraj Tikendrajit Singh, Thangal General and Paona Brajabashi who lost their lives. People started observing 13th August of every year as an anniversary of execution of Jubraj Tikendrajit Singh and Thangal General as both of them was hanged to death on 13th August, 1891. It was observed as the Patriot's Day. There was another date which was observed as the anniversary of the battle of Khongjom. This day was observed as Paona Day or Khongjom Day. There were opinions on the date of the day of Khongjom. According to the *Cheitharol Kumbaba* this date was on 23rd April 1891. There is another opinion of the scholars based mostly on secondary British sources that the battle was fought on 25th April 1891 at Khongjom. The matter became so hot that the Speaker of the Manipur Legislative Assembly appointed an expert committee to decide. The expert committee on the basis of *Cheitharol Kumbaba* and other local sources recommended that 23rd April 1891 was the day when the battle of Khongjom was fought and the Government of Manipur observed 23rd April of every year as the Khongjom day.

There was another group of competent historians who pointed out that the military proceedings in the National Archives of India concerning the military conflict between British forces and Manipur forces of 1891 particularly reports of Captain Rundall who commanded the British forces at the battle of Khongjom clearly recorded that the battle was fought on 25th April 1891. A question had arisen that which date was the true one? It is a methodological issue. *Cheitharol Kumbaba* is an official document; it is not a primary source. The recording of the event was done several months after. It had lost its status of a primary source of information. The military proceedings and the report of Captain Rundall was official and primary source. Captain Rundall was a witness of the battle and he did the fighting himself. This controversy is going on. Whom shall we trust, the primary source of information or the official source of information? The scholars procured records of the military proceedings of 1891 from India Office Library, London. The scholar who did all the research work is a person not less than Pandit N. Khelchandra Singh, the editor of the 1967 edition of *Cheitharol Kumbaba*. He published all these documents in the *Documents of Anglo-Manipur War 1891 Part I and II* (1984, 1991), *Part III* was published by L. Basanti Devi. *Queen Empress vs. Tikendrajit Prince of Manipur: The Anglo-Manipuri Conflict of 1891* was written by John Parratt and Saroj Nalini Parratt (1992). A very thoughtful work on the life of Mrs. Ethel Grimwood was written by Belinda Morse in her *Calamity and Courage: A Heroine of the Raj: The story of Ethel Grimwood in Manipur* published by Book Guild Publishing, Sussex, England in March 2008. The author revisited all the places referred to by Mrs. Ethel Grimwood in her book *My Three Years in Manipur* (1891). Mrs. Morse kindly sent a complimentary copy of this book to the author through a friend, Somi Roy. This is an unknown story of Mrs. Ethel Grimwood after the war of 1891 in Manipur.

This controversy raises the role of the historian and his sources of information. The historian trusted the primary source of information in history.

Another set of writings on modern history of Manipur were carried out by a group of young and modern scholars. They are N. Joykumar's books *From Colonialism to Democracy, History of Modern Manipur, The Social Movements of Manipur and the popular Revolutionary Movements in Manipur*, K. Manimohan's *Hijam Irabot and his Political Movements*", N. Lokendra's *Unquiet Valley* dealing with history of Manipur Valley during the colonial period, Lal Dena's *Colonialism and Christian Mission* deals with British policy towards Manipur and Christian evangelical works in Manipur. His book is a pioneering study. He also edited a centenary publication in honour of Reverend William Pettigrew who was a first Christian missionary in Manipur. It was named, *Reverend William Pettigrew, A Centenary Tribute* (1996).

Learned articles were collected and published by enterprising editors. Mention may be made of *History of Modern Manipur* written by Gangmumei Kamei, Lal Dena and Joykumar Singh under the editorship of Lal Dena. This contributed book had become quite popular. Another contributed work was carried out by Naorem Sanajaoba of Gauhati University who published four volumes of *Manipur: Past and Present*. It was a massive attempt made by scholars of Manipur of different disciplines to write on history, civilization, religion, polity, law and culture of different peoples of Manipur under the hard working editorship of Naorem Sanajaoba. He wrote several works of different subjects. These four volumes have introduced Manipur to India and to the outside world. We may also refer to his *Kunmathoi suba satabdigi Kangleipak puwari* (*History of Kangleipak* of the 21st century).

Another hot historical controversy was the question of merger of Manipur State to Dominion of India. According to a view, Maharaja of Manipur, Bodhchandra Singh was coerced to sign the agreement and Manipur became a part of the Indian Republic. Another view was that it was a popular movement for the merger. There are two works on the subject. Haobam Bhubon Singh a military officer, administrator and political leader published the *Merger of Manipur*. Another counter work known as the *Annexation of Manipur* was published by an activist group. Merger continues to be debated. M. Anandamohan Singh's *Shillong 1949* is autobiographical account of the signing of the Merger Agreement between Maharaja Bodhchandra Singh and the Governor of Assam.

Historical scholarship has been confronted by an extraordinary state of activist interpretation. It is a part of the phenomenon of the intellectual activism which has engulfed the socially conscious elite of Manipur. Historical study has become a multi disciplinary study. Manipur's history has been examined from different angles by the scholars of non-history discipline. This has added new dimensions to historical introspection. One of the consequences of this massive historical exercise is the emerging controversies on almost all landmark historical events, be that sanskritization or desanskritization, the Kabaw Valley issue, the chronology of the battle of Khongjom, Merger Agreement and the Communist movement of Irabot Singh.

We may refer to a well written *The Wounded Land* of John Parratt of Birmingham University. He has written with sympathy on the political, social and economic problems faced by the people of Manipur in the 20th century. He was a passionate spokesman for Manipur in the academic world. I. Mohendra Singh's *The Origin of Meiteis of Manipur and the Meitei-lon is not Tibeto-Burman* (2009) has propounded new theories based on biological findings on origin of man in relation to racial origin of the Meiteis. He also deals with an important chapter on the national character of the Meiteis. His formulation on the origin of the Meitei-lon being a distinctive and indigenous language not related with the century old theory of Tibeto-Burman origin will definitely raise eyebrows among the well established linguistic authorities. One cannot but commend the intellectual efforts of the author.

Ideology in terms of religious and political background has been given a position of primacy. History, historical event and personality have been interpreted to suit the ideology of the different social and political actors. However, the current debate on Merger of Manipur to India in 1949, the political status and the consequences of the merger, the perceived or imagined has gone beyond the parameter of historical inquiry. However, the historical interpretation of events cannot be abandoned by the historians to the activists alone. The truth or facts in historical terminology have to be stated and made known to all concerned Truth cannot be hidden for all time.

Manipur is passing through a critical phase of her history. Historical scholarship is facing a crisis of historical interpretation. There can be use or misuse of history. Historian shall not be and cannot be neutral. He is to be objective and shall stand by the side of the truth. The latest publications is Rajkumar Somorjit Sana's *The Chronology of Meitei Monarchs (From 1666 CE to 1850 CE)* 2010.

Tribal Historiography

There is a reasonable resentment among the hill people of Manipur that their history is not written properly. During the pre-colonial or colonial period, the history of the tribal people was not written as they had not developed the art of writing. However, the tribes both Nagas and the Kuki-Chins have had their oral tradition, myths, legends and genealogy. The tribes belong to, as Levi Strauss says "the society without history". One may not agree with the great French sociologist to describe the tribal or primitive society as society without history. The clan and family genealogies are the important sources of information to reconstruct their history. There is also methodological problem to write the tribal history. Origin, migration and settlement are reconstructed by oral history. The tribes did not develop beyond village level polity. The Naga villages were described by W. McCulloch as the village republics whereas the Kuki-Chin developed village level chieftainship. The history of the relation of these tribes with Meitei state, the Burmese State and British colonial government provided a basis for reconstruction of their history. These relations are recorded in the Meitei chronicles and British administrative records. Many anthropologists and ethnographers reconstructed the history of tribes concerned by using ethno historical method.

In the nineteenth century British officers and historians recorded the ethnography of the tribes, military expedition against the Nagas and influx of Kukis, Lushais and Kanhows in the territory of Manipur. We may refer to R.B. Pemberton, W. McCulloch, Alexander Mackenzie, Robert Brown, Sir James Johnstone who wrote on the Nagas and Kukis. It was McCulloch who gave the classification of the tribes - Nagas and Kukis. However, it was only in the 20th century that the Director of Ethnography of the Government of Assam conducted a systematic ethnographic study of hill tribes of North East India including that of Manipur. We have already referred to *The Meitheis* of T.C. Hodson (1908) regarding the hill tribes, Naga tribes of Manipur was published in 1911 by T.C. Hodson. It was followed by John

Shakespeare's *Lushai Kuki Clans* (1912). Christopher Gimson wrote on *Maring Nagas* (1927). William Shaw wrote on *Notes on Thadou Kukis* (1929). The ethnology of the tribes during colonial period was not so rich. During the post colonial period several monographs were written both by European and Indian scholars. We may mention *Naga Path* written by Ursula Graham Bower (1950). The Naga, Kuki and Meitei scholars of Manipur wrote on several tribes. Mention may be made of M. Horam's *Naga Polity*, and *Socio and Cultural life of the, Nagas*. T.S. Gangte's *Kukis of Manipur* and *Understanding the Kukis*. But history of the tribes on the historical method or ethno-historical method was written by few scholars. A.S. Shimray wrote a *History of Tangkhul Nagas* utilizing the Manipur royal chronicles as sources of history. The most significant work of history of a tribe was written by Gangmumei Kamei. His work *A History of the Zeliangrong Nagas From Makhel to RaniGaidinliu* was written in a true historical form (2004). He also wrote on *Anal - A trans-border Tribe of Manipur* and *Account of the Koireng Tribe*, more or less on ethno-historical method. Lal Dena's *Quest for Identity* is a good work on the Hmar people. H. Kamkhenthang wrote on *Paite - A trans-border tribe*.

Reconstruction of the history of the tribes during the colonial period has been attempted while dealing with the Kuki Rebellion and the Naga Raj Movement. The hill tribes have accepted Christianity and western education had come to Manipur. After the Second World War, there was emerging political consciousness among the hill tribes to protect their interest. The tribal communities started forming their tribal organizations like Tangkhul Long, Kabui Samiti, Manipur Zeliangrong Union, The Kuki National Assembly, The Gangte Tribal Union, The Paite National Council, Khul Union etc. The educated hill tribes got the opportunity to participate in the political process. They entered in the Civil Services and became professionals as teachers, doctors, engineers. Modernization had set in tribal society. The tribal scholars started writing in the tribal dialects and English language on their culture, custom, language, religion and history. There is now developed an incipient historiography and tribal studies.

There grew up insurgency among the Nagas, the Mizos and Kukis. The insurgents started writing history of their movements. Tribal insurgency has become a part of the tribal history. Tribal politics in the democratic process is an aspect of tribal history.

A historiography of the hill tribes could be written both at the state level and tribal level. There are a lot of research going on in the Indian universities and research institutes. A multi disciplinary method based on anthropology, sociology, ethno-history and purely historical method may be utilized to write the tribal history.

FOOT NOTES

1. Herodotus, *The Histories*, translated by A. de Selin court, with an introduction by A. R. Burn, Penguin, 1972.
2. Thucydides, *History of the Peloponnesian War*, translated by Rex Warner with an introduction by M. I. Finlay, Penguin, 1972.
3. Hegel, W.G.F. *Lectures on the Philosophy of World History, Introduction*. Translated by N.B. Nisbet with an Introduction by Duncan Forbes. Cambridge University Press, Cambridge, 1975.
4. Apte, V.S. *English-Sanskrit Dictionary*. History may be translated as *Itihasa, Purabritam, Itihas-Purabrita, Purabhutam* etc.
5. William, Sir Dr. M. Monier, *English-Sanskrit Dictionary*, 1956. There are eighteen *Puranas* and eighteen *Upa Puranas*. The *Puranas* may have historical information but the *Purana* is not history.
6. Thapar, Romila, *Society and Historical Conscience, Itihasa Purana Tradition in History and Beyond*, OUP, p. 151, 2010.
7. Carr, E.H. *What is History?* pp. 31, 62, London, 1962
8. Voltaire, [Francois Marie- Arouet], *Philosophy of History* (1765), the first English Edn. with Preface by Thomas Kiernan, London, 1965.

REFERENCES

Barnes, H.E. *A History of Historical Writings*, New York, 1963.

Bloch, Marc, *Historian's Craft*, London, 1953.

Braudel, Ferdinald, *On History*, London, 1986.

Bury, J.B. *The Idea of Progress: an enquiry into its origin and growth*, New York, 1954.

Carr, E.H. *What is History?* London, 1962.

Collingwood, R.G. *The Idea of History*, London, 1945.

Gardiner, Patrick, *Theories of History*, New York, 1969.

Goel, Dharmendra, *Philosophy of History*, Delhi, 1967.

Hamilton, Paul, *Historicism*, Routledge, London, 1996.

Hegel, W.G.F. *Lectures on the Philosophy of World History* (1822-1830), London, 1975.

Hobsbawm, Eric, *On History*, London, 1997.

Kamei, Gangmumei, *On History and Historiography of Manipur*, Delhi, 2006.

Levi-Strauss, Claude, *Structural Anthropology*, London, 1968

Sen, S.P. (ed.), *Historians and Historiography of Modern India*, Calcutta, 1973.

Spengler, Oswald, *The Decline of the West*, London, 1959.

Subramaniam, N. *Historiography*, Madras, 1974.

Thapar, Romila, *History & Beyond*, Oxford University Press, 2010.

2

Feudalism in Pre-Colonial Manipur

The evolution of a State formation passed through several stages of which feudalism was an important one. It is proposed to examine the feudal elements or tendencies in the polity of pre-colonial Manipur, based on the historical data of nineteenth century. This chapter will examine the characteristics of European feudalism and that of the feudalism in India. We will examine, whether there was feudalism in the history of Manipur. It is proposed to explain the aspects of European Feudalism, Feudalism in India and Feudalism in Manipur.

European Feudalism

According to Marc Bloch (Feudal Society, 1931, 1961) the term feudalism comes from the French *'Feodalite'* (Latin : *Feodum*). It was first used in 1727 by a French scholar named Comte de Boulanviliers in his *Gouvermant Feodal and Feodalite*. It was popularized by an Enlightenment writer Montesquieu by his use of "*Lois Feodalis*" to describe the ancient regime in France. The leaders of the French Revolution were opposed to the feudal regime; and the National Assembly of revolutionary France abolished the Feudal system on 11th August, 1789. Karl Marx in his *Communist Manifesto* (1848) and subsequent writings examined the place of feudalism as a stage of socio-economic formation in Europe. The Marxist writings examine this phenomenon both in theory and practice. Feudalism is located at the third stage of the social, political and economic formulation of European history: primitive communism, slavery based society, feudalism, capitalism and socialism.

Marc Bloch says that feudalism is a type of society and a stage in the social, economic and political development. So it is both a type and a stage of society. Historically, feudalism as a social and political system originated in the western Europe in the middle age. As a category of economic system it preceded the growth of capitalism in Europe. It was basically a system of land tenure, and the rights and privileges attached to it. Under the feudal land tenure, the land belonged to the king. The land grants were given by the monarch to social and political classes: namely, the nobility, clergy, knights, and peasantry including the serfs. The feudal social system was based on the bond of personal relationship amongst the different groups of the feudal hierarchy. But there was the social and political predominance of the land holding aristocracy and the resultant exploitation of the small and weak by the powerful. In the feudal political system, the power of the state was parcellized among groups of the feudal hierarchy; it was weakened and paralyzed by the privileges of the aristocracy.

To the Marxists, feudalism is a pre-capitalist mode of production making it essentially an economic system with social and political ramifications. Feudalism is essentially a European system. But it has been found that institutions similar to it exist among the non-European societies. These are often isolated phenomenon in different frameworks or without inter relationship with the original feudal system. Such fragments of feudal institutions in these countries have been described as feudal tendencies peculiar to that particular country.

According to Marc Bloch, European feudalism consisted of:

> "A subject peasantry, a widespread use of service tenements instead of salary (*fief*), supremacy of the class of specialized warriors, ties of obedience and protection which bind man to man, within the warrior class, assume the distinctive called vassalage; fragmentation of the authority- leading inevitably to the disorder; and in the midst of all this, the survival of other forms of association, family and

state, of which the latter during the second feudal age was to acquire renewed strength such then seem to be the fundamental features of European feudalism" (Feudal Society, p. 446).

Feudalism in India

It is well-known that forms of feudalism existed in non European countries, the ancient Egypt, in Aztec society, Japan and Ottoman Empire. We proceed to analyze the feudalism in India. There is a volume of literature on the historiography of Indian feudalism mostly contributed by the Marxist historians. These are concerned with the exposition of the feudal system in the Medieval India, comparing the Indian feudalism with the European system, and outright rejection of the existence of feudalism in India. The main area of enquiry is the question whether there was feudalism in Indian history culminating in what is known as the Feudalism debate. An overview of the debate is presented by V.K. Thakur in his *Historiography of Indian Feudalism towards a Model of Early Medieval Indian Economy* (1989).

Among the earlier historians who made investigations on the subject mention can be made of D.D. Kosambi who devoted to the existence of feudalism in Indian history. In his *Introduction to the Study of Indian History* (1956), he propounded the concept of feudalism from above and feudalism from below and a comparison of Indian and European system. It was however R.S. Sharma, a well-known historian of ancient India who made a full scale study of the subject in his *Indian Feudalism* (1965). This publication created a flutter of interest in feudalism among historians. B.N.S. Yadava in his *Society and Culture in Northern India in the 12th Century* (1973) made further analysis of Indian feudalism in the middle ages.

However, there are scholars who strongly feel that feudalism did not exist in India. One of them is Irfan Habib, a doyen of medieval Indian historians who outrightly said that according to Karl Marx feudalism did not exist in the pre-colonial India; he also contributed several theoretical analyses on feudalism as a whole. Harbans Mukhia strongly questioned the existence of feudalism in medieval India in his lecture *Was there feudalism in Indian History?*, which was his Presidential address in Indian History Congress in 1979. Harbans Mukhia's lecture was discussed world-wide. It evoked positive responses from the Marxist intellectual world. This lecture and other papers were published in the form of a book edited by Harbans Mukhia himself entitled *The Feudalism Debate* (1999).

Coming back to the Indian feudalism, I refer to Kosambi's concept of feudalism from above and feudalism from below. According to Kosambi, feudalism from above means a state wherein an emperor or a powerful king levied tributes on the subordinates who still in their own rights did what they liked within their own territories as long as they paid the paramount ruler. These subordinate rulers might even be tribal chiefs who once ruled the land by direct administration without the intermediary of a class which was in effect a land owning strata. This category of feudalism from above was found in the formation of most of the Indian states and kingdoms.

Feudalism from below means the next stage where a class of land owners developed, within the village, between the State and peasantry. This class was subject to military service and hence claimed a direct relationship with the state power. Taxes were collected by small intermediaries who passed on a fraction to the feudal lords or the monarch.

Kosambi found some similar characteristics both in European and Indian feudalism like the low level of technology in which the instrument of production was simple and generally inexpensive, the act of production was largely individual in character. The division of labour was at a very primitive level of development. The production of immediate need of a household or a village community and not for a wider market existed in both system. Political decentralization was common to both India and Europe. For example, according to Mauryan theory all land belonged to the king. And the tribal concept of land as a territory but not as a property was held in common by the tribe. This concept existed in both the systems. The holding of land by lords on some kind of service tenure found among the Rajputs whose chief profession was military service and the early Muslim states were found in European system also. R.S. Sharma describes the period between 4th to 13th centuries as feudal period in Indian History. He traces the origin of feudalism in the ancient Indian practice of making land grants to the Brahmins. The result of land grants was the emergence of a class of land lords, living on the produce of the peasants. This was a feudal formation.

R.S. Sharma on Indian Feudalism

R.S. Sharma in his article, *Features of Feudalism in Perspective in Social and Economic History in early India* (1983, 1995) describes the features of the feudal system in early India. The new socio-economic formation was by a sharp differentiation between the peasants and lands and can be regarded as feudal. Sharma noted four main features of the Indian feudalism:

> "First, in a feudal society, there is a basic class of landlords who claim and collect rents from the peasants on the ground that they are the owners of the land. This class was created in India as a result of "the land charters" like the European fiefs.
>
> "Second, the feudal society is primarily based on a class of subject peasantry (like their European counterpart) who is in actual occupation of the land but are compelled to pay rents in cash, kind or labour to the landlords. This situation developed in the country as a consequence of land grants and partly through the power of the local officers".
>
> "Third, the rents and labour services are collected by the landlords who claim the rents and services from the peasants on the basis of land charters granted to them by the monarch. Force is also used by the landlords for collecting the rents etc".
>
> "Fourth, a feudal socio-economic formation originates and grows in a predominantly agricultural economy in which local needs are satisfied locally; and there is little scope for the market. In such a situation, salaries are not paid in cash but in kind. And all kinds of

services such as religious, military, political and administrative etc. are remunerated through the grants of plots of land".

Sharma concludes:

"As a result of continuous land grants, the four features of feudalism in Gupta time became prominent in the period. Socially, this development was accompanied by the proliferation of caste arranged in terms of hierarchy and impurity".

"Thus, the fiscal, military, administrative and religious services were linked to the land grants. The feudal formation created a sharp distinction between the landlords and the peasants, and reinforced the privileges of the princes and clergy by giving them considerable control over the factors of production including land."

Sharma, of course, admitted that there were differences between the Indian and European feudalism. India did not have well defined class of feudal barons. In India, small scale peasants plots were not tied to the large scale landlords forms; there was no regular supply of labour-service by the peasants. There was no system of serfdom in India. There was no manorial system.

Harbans Mukhia on Indian Feudalism

Harbans Mukhia, as noted above raised a number of objections to the exposition of Indian Feudalism. He noted that there were not adequate sources of information on the subject. There was not well organized vassalage regulating the Feudal relations. There was no slavery, no serfdom and no subject-peasantry. After all, feudalism was not a universal mode of production applicable anywhere. Mukhia was of the opinion that if there was no feudalism in India, he was not in favour of Marx's Asiatic Mode of production either.

The debate continues, R.S. Sharma in an article entitled "How feudal was Indian Feudalism" in the *Feudalism Debate* edited by Harbans Mukhia tries to answer the points raised by him. R.S. Sharma admitted that there was variation in the forms of feudalism.

And feudalism was not the monopoly of the western Europe. He sticks to his original position on Indian feudalism. He says:

> "But in spite of the variations, the basic factor, namely the presence of a controlling class of landlords and a subject peasantry, remained the same."

He argues that

> "serfdom should not be considered to be identical with feudalism."

Regarding the subject peasantry, he reiterates that

> "subjection is a characteristic of early medieval Indian social structure."

R.S. Sharma makes the following concluding observation:

> "Feudalism in India, therefore, was characterized by a class of landlords and by a class of subject peasantry, the two living in a predominantly agrarian economy marked by the decline of trade and urbanism and by a drastic cut in metal currency. The superior state got its taxes collected and authority recognized by creating interim power block or even states."

While the debate between the protagonists and opponents on Indian feudalism is not likely to come soon to an end, the fact of the feudal tendencies in Indian state cannot be ignored.

Feudalism in Manipur?

The analysis of the Indian feudalism, of course makes one feel an apprehension whether Manipur variant of feudalism, if any or feudal tendencies existed in pre-colonial Manipur. In this attempt, we will examine the nature of the Meitei monarchy, the Lallup system which was both a military and revenue service rendered to the monarch, the land tenure and the social classes of the pre-colonial Manipur. There were several indigenous sources of information on the political and administrative system of the kingdom of Manipur which was restored to her independence after the Treaty of Yandabo (1826). Manipur was completely devastated during the Burmese conquest (1819-1826). The liberator of Manipur was King Gambhir Singh (1825-1834) who restored the deserted Manipur to its former glory. Five kings of Manipur, Gambhir Singh, Nara Singh, Chandrakirti Singh, Surchandra Singh and Kulla Chandra Singh ruled in Manipur before the British conquest in 1891. The feudal system of Manipur was reconstructed from the sources of history in form of chronicles, historical texts and administrative manuals, supplemented by British official accounts.

Meitei Monarchy

The kingdom of Manipur was a monarchy. The monarch was regarded as the political, social and religious head of the Meitei State. He was given the title of *Meidingu* (lord of the Meiteis). In the ancient times, the Meitei monarchy was weak as it had to struggle with other clan principalities. But after the completion of the establishment of the hegemony over other clan principalities the monarchy had become powerful and claimed supremacy over other clan principalities. It became a highly centralized in the administration. The king was at the top of hierarchy. His court was constituted of the nobility which consisted of royal princes and his favourite officials; another category was the feudatory clan chieftains who accepted his suzerainty and occupied hereditary offices. The king was also assisted by two categories of noble men, one called *Ningthoupongba tara* (ten regional chieftains) and the second was the *Phamdous*. The first category was regarded as a sort of ministers. The second category of nobles, the Phamdous, was selected by the monarch to represent 32 divisions of thc kingdom, two members each from every division. In the seventeenth and eighteenth centuries the king and the Central Government had become more powerful. The king appointed ministers and officials arbitrarily. The nobility was entrusted with several functions, military, civil and judicial works of the state. The apparatus of administration manned by the nobility became very elaborate.

The Meitei State was organized through the *Lallup* service system. There was a well-developed revenue system. The army organization had become powerful through the *Lallup*. Manipur was a poor country with a small population. The economy was based on barter and salaries were paid in kind mostly paddy. The people could not pay taxes to the king but they paid their labour either as a soldier or a development worker. The king gave protection and security for which the people rendered their services. Apart from the existence of a hierarchy of nobility, priestly class, warrior, peasantry and slavery there was no marked characteristic in the administration to call the Meitei State as a feudal monarchy. Some of the characteristics of the Meitei state appear to be feudal.

The most important institution with feudal tendencies in the Meitei state was the *Lallup* system. It was based on the assumption that it was the duty of every male between seventeen to sixty years to place his services at the disposal of the king without the payment of any remuneration for ten days out of forty days. It was an acknowledgement of the king's protection of the country and people. According to tradition it was started by King Pakhangba in the first century A.D. and was abolished by the British in 1892. The *Lallup* service was rendered by all the ethnic groups of Manipur, the Meiteis, the Brahmins and the Muslims known as the Meitei Pangal. In 1735, King Garibniwaz imposed the Lallup on the hill tribes, who were not favourably inclined towards this service.

Lallup System

Lallup was originally a military organization indicated by its name. *Lallup* means war organization (*lal* means war, *lup* means organization). Gradually *Lallup* had extended from military service to non military, developmental works. It was also a revenue service as the people did not pay taxes in cash but in kind in form of paddy. The officials of the State who were engaged in administration were not paid salaries but in form of foodgrains. The military service rendered by the *Lallup* constituted the militia of the Meitei State. The Meitei army before the establishment of the standing army known as the Manipur Levy by King Gambhir Singh in 1824 was constituted of the warriors under the Lallup. The Meiteis were a martial race, a nation at arms. A subject of the Meitei monarchy was essentially a peasant and a warrior who was conversant with martial arts and use of weaponry. He was an infantry man using sword, spear and shields owned by himself. He was a cavalry man having his own horse and equipments consisting of sword, spear, and sling known as arambai. He maintained the horse himself. He was also a boat soldier. The cavalry was well known arm of the army in fighting against neighbouring countries particularly Burmese and Tripuris. It reminds us of the military service rendered by knights of Europe to their suzerain and the king. European knights rendered forty days service in a year to his monarch while the Meitei peasant rendered labour service and military service for eighty days in a year (Ten days out of forty days). The peasant subjects worked during the time of peace, in the royal fields or was engaged in developmental works particularly building roads, bridges, houses for the royal household, carpentry and industrial vocations. The Lallup service was like the corvee of the European system, under which, the European peasant or the serf rendered three days of work for himself and the remaining days for his lord. We find a little similarity between the Lallup system of the Meiteis and feudal services of Europe.

The *Lallup* system was the mainstay of the Meitei State system. It was the personal loyalty of the subjects expressed in form of service rendered to the state. The basis of the *Lallup* service was personal relation between the subjects and the monarch. The Lallup had interconnection with every departments of the government. It was administered through the four administrative divisions known as *Panas*. They were *Ahallup*, *Naharup*, *Khabam* and *Laipham*. The *Pana* system was of unknown origin. During the reign of King Loyamba reference to the *Panas* was made in his royal edict known as *Loyamba Shilyen*. The four *Panas* survived even at the modern times.

In the nineteenth century since the rule of King Gambhir Singh *Lallup* system were put under pressure with the monetization of the economy. Several categories of people were exempted by the king from the *Lallup* dues and obligations. The *Lallup* service could be substituted by payment of money. European observers describe it as force labour. James Johnstone observes:

> "this system known by the name Lallup is often miscalled forced labour…it executed the great public works for the benefit of the state. The system was a good one and when not carried to excess, pressed heavily on nobody. It exceptionally adapted to a poor state sparsely populated. In such a state under ordinary circumstances where the amount of revenue is small and the rate of wages often comparatively high, it is next to impossible to carry on much needed public works by payment. On the other hand, every man in India who lives by cultivation, has much spare time on his hands, and the Lallup system very profitably utilizes this and for the benefit of the community at large. I never heard of it being complained as hardship".

The personal basis of the *Lallup* service indicated the feudal relationship of personal bond between the king and nobles, nobles, warriors and the peasantry.

Land Tenure System

The land tenure system of the Meitei State was fully developed in the eighteenth and nineteenth centuries. The British political agents, officers and ethnographers have left behind adequate reports regarding land tenure system of pre-Colonial Manipur. I would like to refer to the reports of W. McCulloch (1859), Robert Brown (1874), E.W. Dun (1886) and T.C. Hodson (1908). A definitive short account of land revenue system prepared by A.A. Howell, an assistant political officer in Manipur (1891) is a reliable document on revenue system of the pre British period of Manipur history.

The whole land system was based on the assumption that all the land belonged to the king. He was the absolute proprietor of land and natural resources in the kingdom. The king could dispose it of in the way he liked. This concept of the king as the owner and protector of the country, land and natural resources was also prevalent in the state system of Southeast Asia. The king as the greatest land owner endowed with arbitrary power on its utilization was a feudal element in any state system. The revenue department of the state headed by a noble functionary supervised the working of the land tenure. The authority of the state or the kingdom was strengthened by the concept of ownership of the land vested in the king. The present day legal theory that land belongs to the state in Manipur is a legacy of this concept. The land tenure or the ownership of the land could be classified into four categories.

(i) The king and his immediate members of the royal household were the biggest land owner.

(ii) Officers of the state were given lands by the king for their services in lieu of salaries. The favourites of the king were also granted rent free lands.

(iii) Semi-servile peasants who tilled the land on payment of rent.

(iv) The landless slaves who tilled the land on payment of rent to the state.

According to a report made by a British officer the land utilization was based on privileges given by the king. One third of the land was given by the king to his nobles and officers who paid the rent in kind. This category of land was known as Phamlou. Second one third of the land was given by the king to his royal relatives, the Brahmins, the soldiers (sepoys) and other favourites. The remaining one third was leased to the peasants. Slaves were also given tenure to cultivate either royal lands or nobles land on payment of high rent. It was estimated that there were about 1200-1500 slaves were employed in the pre British period.

Land Grants

The king gave grants of land to officers and nobles for distinguished services, to the Brahmins and temples for their maintenance and king's reward for his favourites. The land grants were categorized as follows:

Manalou

Rewards of paddy fields were given in recognition of a person's contribution to the king or the state and such lands were known as *manalou* (*mana* = reward, *lou* = paddy field). The tenure was for lifetime of the grantee. The manalou holders constituted a major social class that strengthened or weakened the ruling group in the State.

Brahminlou (Brahmin Land)

This category of land grant was given to the Brahmin at the time of performance of the sacred thread ceremony (*lugun*). This was also popularly known as *lugunlou* (land of the sacred thread). A Brahmin received a *pari* (hectare) of land from the king as a customary gift.

Temple land

This kind of land grant was known as *lailou* (land for the deities). The lands were granted for the maintenance of Hindu temples and *Umanglais* (village deities) for their maintenance. The temple of God Govindaji which was the temple of the royal family was granted hundred *paris* of land and these lands were cultivated by the slaves. The land granted to the *Umanglais* was looked after by the community.

Sanalou (Royal Lands)

Members of the royal family were also granted lands. This was known as *sanalou*. In 1891, the queen of Manipur possessed 600 hectares of land. The members of the royal family were biggest land owners in the kingdom.

Pangallou

The persons of distinguished service in war were granted such lands. *Pangallou* holders were normally the favourites of the king.

In 1891, it was reported that there were only two hundred persons holding the *Pangallou.*

Lands as Salary

The officials and the soldiers were given lands in lieu of salary. *Phamlou* was the term used for the land held in connection with some office. This land was the salary given to the holders of the office. The revenue payable was one pot of paddy (two baskets of paddy) per *pari*. The members of the armed forces known as the sepoys (*siphai*) in the nineteenth century were given the siphailou for their military services. The following was the rate of salaries payable in land.

A *Menjor* received one *pari* of land for each company he commanded in a regiment known as *Tuli*, a *Poila* got six *paris*, a Subedar, four *paris*, a Jemadar, three *paris*, a Kut, 2.5 *paris*, a Havildar, two *paris*, a Amaldar, one *pari*, Kotendar, 1.5 *paris*, a Sepoy, 1.25 *paris*

The sepoys were not entitled to any pension but after his death two *sangams* of land were given to his son(s).

Lands for the Community

The community lands included community forests surrounding the village, the grazing grounds and play fields.

The above description shows that the land tenure in Manipur was highly stratified almost on the lines of feudal classes. However, the *zamindari* system did not emerge. A rapid analysis of three institutions of the Meitei state, the Monarchy, the *Lallup* and land tenure would show some feudal tendency but it was not a clear cut feudal system.

The Structure of the Meitei State

The structure of the State covers the nature of the monarchy, the bureaucratic set up of the government, administration of justice, revenue and military services. The structure shows that monarchy was the form of the Meitei State system. The concept of the Meitei kingship had a mythical origin. It was based on the myth or legend of the contest between the two divine sons of the Divine Lord of the Universe, Atiya Guru *Shidaba* (Immortal Lord of the sky) for the throne of their divine father. The two brothers were Sanamahi and Pakhangba. In the contest, the younger Pakhangba outwitted his more capable elder brother, Sanamahi due to the machination of their mother Goddess Leimaren. There ensued a fight between the two brothers. The divine father settled the dispute. Sanamahi would be worshipped in every household and Pakhangba was made the king and a royal deity of the human world. Pakhangba took residence at Kangla, a holy place of the Meitei religion, culture and seat of power.

Kangla was regarded in the mystical Meitei world as the navel of the earth and the centre of the universe. The concept of the royal palace and capital as the centre of the world existed in the Burmese state also. Kangla was the core of the Meitei state. Historically, the royal chronicle, Cheitharol Kumbaba, records that the first historical king who was the founder of the Ningthouja dynasty (A.D.33 to 1891 or 1949) who ruled at Kangla was Nongda Lairen Pakhangba. Every ruler of Manipur claimed descent from Pakhangba though the chronicles ascribed to him a divinity, he was a human being. Later rulers believed that the king of Ningthouja dynasty was an incarnate of the god Pakhangba who presided over the Kangla. Pakhangba was given the title of *Meidingu* (the Lord of the Meitei). He was also descended as the lord of the seven clans of the Meitei (*Mayum Taret Ki Piba*, lord of the seven houses or clans).

Unless a king performed the coronation ceremony (*Phambal Kaba*) he was not recognized as the king. There are historical treatises on the coronation ceremonies. We may refer to the two texts: *Pakhangba Phambal* and *Naothingkhong Phambal Kaba*. Rituals, coronation costumes and the process of the ceremony are described.

The Ningthouja King combined in himself the position of social head, political and religious head and commander in-chief. In the ancient period, the king was not that powerful. In the 17th and 18th centuries, King Khagemba (1597-1652) and the Hinduised Garibniwaz (1709-48) claimed the divine status. It was indicated by two assertions. Khagemba assumed the title of *Lainingthou* (Godly King). Garibniwaz was declared to be an incarnate of Hindu God, Lord Vishnu. Divinity of the Meitei King, as god, an incarnate of Lord Pakhangba and Lord Visnu was asserted in later period. A prince belonging to the line of *Nongdalairen Pakhangba*, while performing the coronation ceremony at the Kangla could become the King (*Ningthou* or *Ningthourel*) with the political support from the clan chiefs and divine sanction of Lord Pakhangba. Whoever occupied the Kangla would be the ruler.

The kings of Manipur assumed the title of "Maharaja" after their conversion into Hinduism. The title of "Raja" was of an inferior rank and was given by the British in 1891. Every king was given a regnal title (*Phambal Minghul*) at the performance of a mock coronation battle known as *Phambal lal*. Sometimes a king was named after a victory over the enemy like *Khagemba* (conqueror of the Chinese) or *Kyamba* (conqueror of the Shan principality known as Kyang). The kings were given, after conversion to Hinduism two titles, a Meitei title and a Sanskrit name. *Pakhangba* was also named Yavishta, Garibniwaz was known as Pamheiba and Gopal Singh.

The Royal Court

Theoretically, the king was the head of the state; he was the source of all power, a fountain of justice and the head of the army. Sometimes he acted as a chief priest of the country during the performance of state rituals. He was the source of all honour and rewards. However, the king's power was greatly limited by the customs and traditions of the Meiteis known as Chatlam Lutin which was a sort of common law. These customary laws were interpreted and administered by the nobles who constituted the court of the king. The king was the pivot of the administration, all departments circling around him. N. Ibobi Singh observes, "He was not an autocrat". T.C. Hodson agreed:

> "the centre of the state was the Raja. He himself took no direct part in the administration except on formal occasion when he presided over the Durbar (court)."

The king was assisted in the running of the government by the officers of the court who were appointed by him. There were two unique institutions or the organs of the court which were vital in the process of decision making and in the implementation of the decision by the government. The first one was called *Ningthou Pongba Tara* (ten regional chieftans) and the other was called the Phamdous. A writer describes the Ningthou Pongba Tara as a council of ministers, while another scholar called the institution of the sixty four Phamdous as an assembly of the kingdom. The Ningthou Pongba Tara is referred to in the myth of *Numit Kappa* (shooting of the sun) which gives a narrative of slave rebellion against two brother kings. (According to the myth a Khaba rebel shot the king who went into hiding leaving behind anarchy in the land. No king and no kingdom. Through the intervention of ten regional gods, a compromise was made; the king was recalled to the throne, the rebel was made a noble and the ten gods or chiefs were enjoined to assist the king in the administration in the Meitei country). The myth refers to the ten gods (*Nongpok, Chingkhei, Wangpurel, Khana Chaoba, Thangjing, Sampurel, Loyarakpa, Koubru* and *Marjing*) who were the precursors of the ten noble chiefs.

The historical *Ningthou Pongba Tara* were the regional chiefs who became the nobles in the court of Meitei kings. Their names were the following: *Pukhranba, Nongthonba, Hiyangloi Hanjaba, Chongkhanba Hanjaba, Imingloi Hanjaba, Imangloi Hanjaba, Khwailakpa, Yaiskullakpa, Naikhulakpa, Phamtakcha.* There were changes made in the list of posts in the reign of different kings. The standard names of the post which existed as late as 1907 were *Nongthonbam, Pukhranba, Wangkheilatpa, Yaiskullatpa,*

Khurailatpa, two Shanglenlatpas and two Shangkhulatpas. We do not know how they were designated before the rule of Garibaniwaz during whose time the designation of mantri (ministers) was adopted. The chronicles and inscription testify to this. Therefore the *Ningthou Pongba Tara* were the traditional posts in the court having equivalence to Mantri (in Sanskrit) and minister (in English). In the nineteenth century, there were the posts of the ministers designated as *mantri*. The word, '*Patramantris*' are used in the chronicles.

Phamdous: A Council or Assembly of the Nobles?

The *Phamdous* were the nobles who were appointed by the king to be the members of his court. The role of a Phamdou was general and all embracing. The royal chronicle refers to the post of *Phamdou*. They were the most influential group in the process of decision making in the Meitei state. There were sixty four *Phamdou*. They were appointed to represent 32 divisions covering 172 villages according to Khanthok Nipan Lamyanba, a historical text quoted by N. Ibobi Singh. The king appointed a permanent person generally a knowledgeable commoner to represent one division. Another assistant was also appointed to assist him. There were two *Phamdou* from each of the thirty two divisions making them to 64 *Phamdou*.

The functions of *Phamdou* were more or less consultative. They were a strong lobby in the court as they acted in group. In most cases they raised objection to arbitrary action of the king. In the later years the king started appointing their relatives or favourites as *Phamdou*. We do not have adequate sources of information on the working of institution of *Phamdou*. A learned scholar Nandalal Sharma argued that it was an assembly of the representatives of people in the royal courts. How far was the *Phamdou* a democratic representative? We do not know. But the stray references to their function indicate a similarity to the Anglo-Saxon institution of the Witan, the assembly of the nobles in feudal England. It is not sure whether they should be regarded as the council or assembly of the representatives of the people. True, the *Phamdous* were representatives of the thirty two divisions in the valley section of Manipur. The royal chronicle records several anecdotes in which the *Phamdou* were involved. There were instances of corruption of the royal judicial officers. In order to deal with critical situations *Phamdous* were entrusted by the kings to solve the problem.

Government Departments

The government of the Manipur kingdom aimed at the protection of the life and property of the subjects of the kingdom, defence of the territory and collection of revenues in cash and kind to finance the government. Therefore, the number of functional departments was few in the early period, but they grew in number with the expansion of the state activities, and increase in the population due to immigration and conquest and the need to maintain a military establishment and foreign relation.

The core departments were the war department (*lalmi loishang*), finance (revenue) department, home (police and jail) department (*dolai paba loishang*) and *awapurel* (department of foreign affairs). The welfare departments included *pandit loishang* (department of astrologer and pandits), *konung loishang* (royal household), Govindaji temple, *haomacha loishang* (department of Naga), *urungba* (department of forest), *lourungshang* (department of revenue), *pangal loishang* (Muslim affairs), *ametpa* and *maiba loishang* (medical department), *sinnaiba loishang* (department of works), *singsaroi* (department of builders etc.). There were sixteen departments in the 19th century.

War Department

The war department was called lalmi loishang. The army consisted of infantry, cavalry, boat, elephant corps (*shamutongba*), transport (*pothang*). The war weapons of the infantry were home made, sword, spear, shield, sling (*arambai*). Other sophisticated weapons like guns were manufactured in the royal workshops. The army was organized on the *Lallup* system. It was a militia constituted of the peasant soldiers who rendered the fuedal service to the king. The *Lallup* based militia (*lalmi*) was replaced by a standing army, organized on British line by Gambhir Singh onwards.

Police Department

Though the general law and order were maintained by the king through the different officials, a separate department of police was established during the reign of Khagemba. They were known as the *Dollai Paba*. Their functions were to catch stray cattle, capture slaves, punish convict prisoners and to go on errands of the officials. During the reign of Chandrakanta Singh the post of the Kotowal was established to deal with police and jail affairs.

Finance Department

It was most important of all the departments. The finance department worked under the supervision of Nongthonba, a minister in-charge of financial affairs. He was assisted by a number of officials known as *shellungba*. The department consisted of land settlement and land records and collection of revenues and kinds. The department of lourungshang was the head of the land settlement. He also looked after the collection of revenues under the Lallup system, salt taxes, hard tax, fisheries and minting of currency.

Department of Foreign Affairs

It was called awapurel, a department created during the reign of Chandrakirti Singh to look after the Burmese affairs and boundary disputes.

Pandit Loishang

It was the department of pandits and maichous, which was first used during the reign of Charairongba. The functions of the pandit loishang were to look after the traditional educational system, to record the royal chronicles, to engrave important events on stones and copper plates and to act as a guardian of the social customs of the Meiteis. The office of the *Leirikyengbam* (scribes) was attached to the pandit loishang. They wrote down the order of the kings and drafted the answer to the foreign letters. The scholars of the *pandit loishang* acted as guide, teacher and friend of the villagers.

The Sinnaiba Loishang

The *sinnaiba loishang* was the department of works which had 18 sections which over activities like painting (ayekpa), turnering (*phundrei*), blacksmithy (*thangja hanba*), brass making (konsang), tailoring (*phurit saba*), tannery (*nandeiba*), boat making (*hishaba*), mosquito nets (*kabo phurit saba*), drum making etc.

Payment to the Government Employees

No fixed remuneration or salary was paid. Since *Lallup* was the basis of the administration they were not given salaries in cash but only lands by the State. The peasants in turn gave revenue in form of paddy. The grades of remuneration were elaborately fixed.

Administrative Divisions

In the early period, there was no clear cut administrative division. The area represented by a *Phamdou* consisted of specific names of villages under a supervisor, was not based on any geographical or territorial demarcation. Traditionally the kingdom had four territorial divisions: *Ahallup*, *Naharup, Laipham* and *Khabam*, believed to have been established during the reign of King Pakhangba. Loiyamba established six divisions known as Lup according to the royal chronicle. The *Loiyamba Shilyen* edited by Kh. Chandrashekhar and translated by N. Sanajaoba refers to six *panas* adding two more, *Hitakphanba* and *Potshangba*. The names of the divisions were different: *Lup* and *Pana*, but the function might be similar. During the zenith of Manipur's power, we have a fully developed *Pana* system.

Pana became an important aspect of administration affecting the social and cultural life. *Lallup* was organized on the *Pana* basis. Somebody described it a district or a county of England. All the departments, all services, military, revenue collection, religious affairs, sports and cultural activities were organized on the *Pana* system. Of the six panas importance was given to the panas of Ahallup and Khabam. The new panas of Hitakphanba and Potshangba were given less importance. Many tribal villages and Loi villages were not covered by pana system. Taxes and tributes were given by them direct to the king. The village continued to be an important unit of administration. The village had several leikais which were organized into Keirup and Shinglup.

Administration of Justice

In the ancient times, justice was administered by the king himself from whom emanated the judicial power. The king was the fountain of justice. Later on several courts were established to deal with several categories of cases like non religious matters, civil and criminal cases by the chief court, Cheirap, lower courts, Waiyen Kati and Kuchu.

The religious cases were dealt with by the Pandit Loishang and Brahma Sabha. Women affairs were dealt with by the women's court known as the Paja. The military cases were handled by the military court known as the Top garod.

The Cheirap Court

The Cheirap was the highest court of the land. It dealt with both civil and criminal cases. It was both an original court and court of appeal. The court consisted of fifty three members including twenty four ex-officio members. The court was presided over by the Angom Ningthou who was originally the chief of Angom clan occupying a feudatory position in the Ningthouja court since the time of Pakhangba. The important members were:

1. *Angom Ningthou*,
2. *Yuvraj* (the heir apparent),
3. Four ministers namely, *Wangkheilakpa, Khurailakpa, Yaiskullakpa* and *Khwairakpa*,
4. Chiefs of *Panas, Laiphamlakpa, Ahallup Lakpa, Khabam Lakpa, Naharup Lakpa*,

5. Ministers like *Pukhranba, Nongthonba,*
6. Clan chiefs like *Luwang Ningthou* (chief of Luwang clan), *Moirang Ningthou* (chief of Moirang),
7. *Shanglenpuba, Shanguba* and *dewans* of four *panas*.

Wayen Kati

Wayen Kati was a grade of rural court located in the villages.

Pandit Loishang and Brahma Sabha

The religious and customary cases were settled by the *Pandit Loishang* which had knowledgeable scholars to settle such matters. They belonged to the seven clans. The *Brahma Sabha* consisting of the Brahmin scholars dealt with the cases connected with Hindu rites, rituals and customs of the followers of Hinduism. These two institutions continued upto modern times. The British did not interfere in the working of these offices. Brahma Sabha became oppressive during the colonial period.

Women Court

Paja (*Pacha*) was the court dealing with women affairs. The chronicle says that Queen Laisna wife of King Pakhangba was the first judge of this women court. It dealt with family disputes and adultery. The head of the court was called *Paja Hanba.*

The Military Court

Top Garod was the military court. The Senapati was the chief of the Top Garod which consisted of commanders of the army regiments. It decided on the military cases. Appeal could be made to the Cheirap court.

The Social Classes

The Meitei society was not a stratified society during the pre-Hindu days. It was a casteless and the classless society. With the growth of the administrative hierarchy, the holders of the administrative posts emerged as a class; the members of the royalty, the nobles, civil and military officials, the soldiers and the peasants.

After Sanskritization, the Hindu Meiteis were declared as Kshatriya caste. The immigrant Brahmins speaking the Manipuri language and marrying Meitei women formed themselves a caste outside the Meitei society.

The descendents of former kings and princes, were named the Raj Kumars who formed a class of the Meitei society. They were the privileged social class. The outcastes of the Meitei society due to their social and religious crimes formed the low caste of the Hindu society. The hill tribes and the Muslim were outside the Meitei society. But many of them took up State employment. In the nineteenth century, the Hindu Kshatriya caste who became the officials of the State was integrated into a feudal class. The king and the feudal nobles ruled the kingdom with the help of the Brahmins.

Brahmins controlled the *Brahma Sabha*. They played important role in the administration and religious life of the kingdom. Slavery was also in existence for many centuries. The slavery system was mild. The practice of manumission was also in existence.

The royalty and nobility gave importance to feudal etiquettes Ranks of the nobility were indicated by the privileges to ride a palanquin, wear certain turban, cloths and dresses by male or female members. Sartorial system of the bureaucracy was a highly articulated dress code. Over and above this, there were personal bonds between the king, queens and the princes with nobility. Social classes came out of the state officialdom. Everybody tried to hold some office big or small. The office was acquired through feudal favouritism rooted in royal power. Corruption and inefficiency were also rampant in the declining feudal state. Feudal values, feudal mannerism, religious and social orthodoxy, and feudal favouritism were the features of the feudal state and society in Manipur.

With this brief enquiry into the existence, or otherwise of the feudal elements in the structure of the Meitei state in the pre-colonial period of history of Manipur, it is clear that feudalism in the European form did not exist in Manipur. However, the feudal elements and feudal nuances were found in the structure of the polity and the societal relationship in society during the nineteenth century.

REFERENCES

Bloch, Marc: *The Feudal Society* Vol I & II, London, 1939.

Brown, R. *A Statistical Account of Manipur*, Calcutta, 1874.

Chandrasekhar, Kh. (Ed): *Loiyamba Shilyen*, Imphal, 1984.

Chandrashekhar, Kh. Mashil, Imphal. 1997.

Dun, E.W. *Gazetteer of Manipur*, Shimla, 1886.

Higgins, J.C. : *Notes on Meithei (Manipuri) Beliefs and Customs*, Edited by John Parrat, Imphal, 1998.

Hodson, T.C. *The Meitheis*, London, 1908.

International Encyclopedia of Social Science: Vol V, 1972 on Feudalism, Joshua Prawar and Samuel N Eisenstadt, pp 393-402.

Johnstone, James: *My Experience in Manipur and Naga Hills*, London, 1896.

Kamei, Gangmumei : *A History of Manipur: A Pre-Colonial Period*, Vol. I, National Publishing House, New Delhi, 1991 and 2004 Edn.

Kamei, Gangmumei: From Tribalism to Feudalism: Evolution of the Meitei State in Pre-Colonial Manipur, *Professor H.K. Barpujari, Endowment Lecture 2009* published by North Eastern India History Association, Shillong, 2010.

Kamei, Gangmumei: *Presidential Address: State Formation in North East India : A review,* North East India History Association 1986, Kohima Session.

Khelchandra , N. (Edn): *Phamlon, Manipur* Sahitya Parishad, Imphal, 1997.

Kosambi, D.D. *An Introduction to the study of Indian History*, Bombay, 1975, 1988 (Revd Edn).

Leontyev, L. *Pre-Capitalist Modes of Production n Political Economy*, 1972, Moscow.

MacKenzie, Alexander: *A History of Relation of the Hill Tribes with the Government of all North Eastern Frontier of Bengal*, 1884, Calcutta (relevant portion).

McCulloch, W. *An Account of Valley of Munnipore,* Calcutta, 1859.

Mclallan, David: *Karl Marx, Selected Writings*, Oxford University Press, 1977, 2000 (2nd Edn), 2001 (Reprint).

Mukhia, Harbans : *The Feudal Debate*, 1999, Delhi.

Roy, J. *A History of Manipur*, Calcutta, 1958.

Sharma, Nandalal: *Meitrabak*, Imphal, 1960.

Sharma, R.S. *Indian Feudalism*, 1965, 1980 (Revd Edn).

Sharma, R.S. *Material Culture and Social Formation in Ancient India*, Macmillan, Delhi, 1983, 2000 (Reprint).

Sharma,R.S. *Perspective to Social and Economic History of Early India*, 1983, 1995 (Revd Edn).

Singh, Ch. Manihar (Ed): *Naothingkhong Phambal Kaba* (in English tranaslation), Imphal, 1986.

Singh, L. Chandramani: *Manipur Itihas* (in Manipuri) Imphal, 1970.

Singh, L. Iboongohal: *An Introduction to Manipur*, Imphal, 1960.

Singh, L.M.I. and Pandit N Khelchandra Singh: *The Cheitharol Kumbaba*, 1st Edn, 1967.

Singh, N. Ibobi: *The Manipur Administration (1709-1907),* Imphal, 1976, 2003 (Reprint).

Singh, N. Joykumar: *From Colonialism to Democracy, A Modern History of Manipur*, Guwahati.

Singh, N. Lokendra: *Unquiet Valley,* Mittal Publications, New Delhi, 1996.

Singh, R.K. Jhalajit: *A Short History of Manipur*, Imphal, 1965.

Singh, R.K. Sanahal: *Manipur Itihas*, Imphal, 1947.

Thakur, V.K. *Historiography of Indian Feudalism towards a Model of Early Medieval Indian Economy*, Delhi, 1989.

Yaima, Kh. (Ed): *Pakhangba Phambal*, Imphal, 1967.

3

Colonial Policy and Practice

The British Colonial Rule

The British conquered Manipur in 1891 and they ruled the State till 1947. The British imposed their supremacy and paramountcy on Manipur State. There were three aspects of British colonial rule; the first was that Manipur was not annexed to British India and was restored to a young prince of a former ruling family and a direct British rule for 16 years during which the British Indian pattern of administration was introduced. The second was that of a princely State over which was imposed the feudal rule of the Raja with the help of a Manipur State Durbar with its jurisdiction confined on the small valley of Manipur. The third was the administration of the hill tribes under the British Political Agents.

Colonialism or colonial rule was a historical phenomenon: conquest, emigration and subjugation happened in history. Colonialism is the establishment and maintenance for an extended term of rule over an alien people that is separate from and subordinate to the ruling power. Colonialism means domination of an alien minority, administrators, business men and soldiers asserting their racial and cultural superiority over the subjugated people. European colonialism had passed through three phases of historical development: Mercantilism, *laissez faire* and protectionism. Mercantilism was the exploitation of the colonies for the benefit of mother countries; *laissez faire* or Free Trade meant free competition coupled with liberal ideas of utilitarianism and social Darwinism. Protectionism meant the policy of protection of the economic and commercial interest of a colonial power facing rivalry from similar powers. The colonial powers including the British gave up free trade policy and were inclined more towards protectionism. The British imperial expansion in India was completed in the end of the 19th century. Protectionism and liberalism were behind this imperial expansion. It coincided with the British conquest of north eastern India including Manipur.

Colonial Policy

A colonial policy was the general principle followed by a colonizing power to regulate the colonial relationship between her and her dependency. A colonial policy would have political, economic, cultural, social and moral objectives for the attainment or maintenance of which administrative machinery was created to work in the colony. But a colonial relationship involved two social systems, two or more cultural patterns, two civilizations, two different levels of technology and economy, a colonial policy was designed with the deeper connotation and implications. Ideas, ideology, interest and social norms were built in to a colonial policy. Therefore, "a colonial policy means the framing of a social order that provides for an acceptable *modus vivendi* in an oriental society wherein, the westerners have penetrated, have settled and are carrying on business."[1]

Colonial Objectives

The objectives of the colonial policy were implemented through the administrative machinery which was created to administer the colonies. The art and practice of colonial administration was a highly specialized part of the government. During the mercantilist era, the great chartered companies built up administrative cadres to administer the colonies and the administration was geared at the exploitation of colonies for the benefit of the mother countries. The primary concern of a colony, then, was to act as a source of raw materials and market for the finished products of the industries of the mother country. The functions of the colonial administration had become elaborate.

The scope of the colonial administration was related to the objectives of the colonial policy. Since a colony was to be a source of raw material, a market and in some as a place of industrial enterprise especially plantation industry, the administration aimed at obtaining three main objectives; to maintain law and order, to collect revenues through a well formulated taxation system to meet the cost of administration and to adjudicate judicial matters. Therefore, the administration's function covered the army and police for defence, conquest and to keep internal order to ensure stability in the colony; then an elaborate system of fiscal administration. The civil service was to administer both the law of the colonizing power and law of the indigenous people. A well conceived judicial system was the primary step in the administration of a settled civil government.

The colonial administration was influenced by the liberal ideas of utilitarianism. And it adopted welfare programmes. The colonial administration in Manipur also utilized the services of the Christian missionaries to legitimize their rule over the conquered people and to facilitate the westernization of the indigenous tribal society.

The Policy of Indirect Rule

The British policy towards the native States of India during the rule of the British was described as a *policy of indirect rule*. India under the British was divided in to two forms of administration. One was British India, the other group was native States of India subordinate to British paramountcy. The term "Indirect Rule" was mentioned by F.S. Furnivall in describing the British rule over the Shan States of Burma. He developed the concept of indirect rule to explain the relation between the British Indian Empire and the native States of newly conquered province of Burma. This concept was further developed by John Hurd II[2] to describe the nature of British rule and control over the kingdoms which were described as princely or native States.

According to John Hurd II, in India a sizeable part of the country was governed under a system of indirect rule. The indirect rule was differentiated with British India which was ruled by the colonial government. The British India had a single ruler, the Viceroy and one bureaucracy named Indian Civil Service which was responsible to the Viceroy. The army controlled by the highest military command consisted of British officers and native soldiers.

The indirect rule was imposed on the native States. Some salient features are elaborated by John Hurd are as follows:

(i) The so-called native States, having no control over their external affairs which were conducted by the British had considerable autonomy in the internal affairs.

(ii) They passed and administered their own laws, levied their own taxes and maintained their own bureaucracy and police

(iii) The civil servants of such a State served the particular princely State and were responsible to the ruler. The State officials were locally educated. Rulers, officials and subjects alike were linked by marriage, caste and religious bonds. The social and educational ties made the ruling members of the State locally oriented.

(iv) The laws were mostly local and extended only to the State's boundaries.

(v) Public borrowing capacity of a State was limited to its own credit rating. Public borrowing in British India and in Great Britain for the States was discouraged.

John Hurd II further argued that the States were autonomous theoretically. The British sent representatives to the States. They were to observe scrupulously the tradition and customs of the State concerned. However, *de facto*, the position of a State was not so clear. He pointed out that

(i) The Government of India interfered in the internal affairs of the States in varying degrees of the particular State; its history, current condition and personality of the rulers.

(ii) British interference was carried out in many ways. When a prince abused his subjects, defaulted on his credit or violated the wishes of the government, the British could depose him

(iii) The succession to the throne was subject to the approval of the British Government. If a ruler was deposed or a prince was a minor, the British took over the administration of the State

(iv) The native States undertook no major reforms. And they were allowed to retain their distinctive political character which was different from that of British India.[3]

The policy of indirect rule was introduced in the native State of Manipur with certain variation.

Churachand Singh as the Raja of Manipur

The British forces occupied Imphal on 27th April, 1891. The Government of India appointed Major H.P. Maxwell as the Political Officer during the expedition. He was also appointed as the Political Agent and Superintendent of the State of Manipur. Lord Lansdowne, the Viceroy and Governor-General was deeply involved in the affairs of Manipur. He was concerned with the future of Manipur State. Her Majesty, Queen Victoria was concerned with the impact of the conquest of Manipur on princely States of India. She tried to intervene to rescue Prince Tikendrajit Bir Singh from death sentence. The press in India and England publicized Quinton's expedition to Manipur and the trial of the princes. The *Amrita Bazar Patrika* and other Bengali papers of Calcutta expressed sympathy with the Manipur king and his brothers. In England, the Times were critical of Government of India's policy and action towards Manipur. Some of its editorials expressed the sane opinion of English public. The London *Illustrated Weekly News* published a number of paintings and photos of the officers, places and events of Manipur. The British Parliament also discussed the affairs of Manipur. The Government of United Kingdom particularly the Secretary of State was critical of action of Government of India, though they gave open support to the Viceroy on this affair. Queen Victoria, in her journal recorded her unhappiness towards the Indian Civil Service and impact of Manipur affairs on other princely States of India.[4] Therefore, the Government of India took a special care in arriving at a policy towards Manipur. The policy was put in practice during their rule of 56 years.[5]

The first policy decision made by the British Indian Government, after the conquest of Manipur was the future of the State of Manipur; annexation of the State in to British India as a punishment for Anglo-Manipur war or restoration of the kingdom to a prince belonging to the family of the ex-Maharaja or a collateral line of the ruling family. In an answer to a discussion in British Parliament, Lord Viscount Cross, the Secretary of State for India announced that the Government was not in favour of annexation of Manipur and the introduction of British rule in the State. Viceroy Lord Lansdowne was an imperialist par excellence. He was aware of the impact of such a policy of annexation on the princely States. He knew that Queen Victoria was not in favour of further annexation of a princely State to the Indian Empire. In a minute, Lord Lansdowne raised two pertinent questions: (i) whether the kingdom of Manipur revolted against the Queen, and if so the kingdom was liable to penalty which might be in form of payment of indemnity, payment of tribute or annexation of the territory, (ii) did the British Government have the moral right to annex such a conquered territory in the light of the Queen's Proclamation of 1858 in respect of recognition of the princely States in India? These issues were discussed by the Governor General in Council. Legal opinions were expressed that the government of a princely State did not have the right to revolt against the Government of India. If there was a revolt against the Queen, the British government had the right to punish the princely State. The Governor General in Council decided that Manipur had waged a war against the Queen and so she ought to be punished. The Governor General decided that the Government of India had the moral right to annex a conquered territory of the princely State that had revolted.

However, Lord Lansdowne was not in favour of annexation by way of punishment. The opinion among the Anglo-Indian bureaucracy in India was in favour of annexation, which would lead to the obliteration of the State of Manipur as a political entity. Therefore, it was decided to elicit the opinion of the Chief Commissioner of Assam and the British Political Agent in Manipur with whom Lord Lansdowne was in communication. Sir William Ward, the new Chief Commissioner of Assam following him Major H.P. Maxwell the Political Agent of Manipur who represented the hard liner among the Indian Civil Service towards Manipur affairs, were asked to submit their comments for a policy decision by the Government of India. William Ward in consultation with Major Maxwell recommended that the Government of India were justified in annexing the State (for the maintenance of the British prestige) and to teach a lesson and warning to other native States of India. The hill people being one third of the total population of Manipur would welcome the annexation. The British were obliged to protect the hill people of the State against oppression by the king. It was a moral duty imposed upon the British to annex Manipur. From financial point of view also, there were no grounds for thinking that the annexation would result in to financial loss.

This proposal of the Chief Commissioner, Ward was turned down and he was directed to make another proposal who would be the ruler in case of the restoration of the State. Chief Commissioner Ward directed Political Agent Maxwell to prepare three genealogical tables of (i) descendents of King Garibniwaz (1709-1748), (ii) successors of Maharaja Gambhir Singh (1825-1834) and (iii) descendents of Maharaja Nara Singh (1844-1850). In consultation with the local scholars, Major Maxwell submitted the tables. He also suggested that if annexation were rejected and restoration was to be brought about, the son of ex-Maharaja Surchandra Singh might be considered for the post of the Raja. William Ward endorsed this opinion but Viceroy rejected it. It was further directed to indicate the living descendents of the family of Maharaja Nara Singh. Major Maxwell searched out the family of Raj Kumar Chaubi Yaima who had left behind two wives and six children. His first wife had four sons of whom Churachand Singh was the youngest and a minor of 5 years. Chief Commissioner Ward suggested two names; the son of Surchandra Singh named Sur Singh, a twelve-year prince who was not involved in the recent rebellion and Churachand Singh, a surviving descendent of the collateral line of Maharaja Nara Singh. Sur Singh or Churachand Singh was to be chosen for the rulership of Manipur. It was considered that Churachand, a minor boy would be free from the influence of descendents of the ex-Maharaja. Thus the final decision was made by the Governor-General in Council:

i) It was decided not to annex the State.

ii) It was decided to choose Churachand Singh, a great grandson of Maharaja Nara Singh to be the ruler of Manipur.

iii) The British Government would directly manage the administration of Manipur during the minority of new Raja. Major Maxwell, the Political Agent and the Superintendent of the State would administer Manipur.

The case was eventually settled by the issue of the following Proclamation and Notification:

> "the selected ruler Chura Chand was a child of five years of age, distant collateral of the ex-Maharaja, and the youngest of several brothers."

A proclamation was issued on 21st August 1891 which stated:

> "Whereas the State of Manipur has recently been in armed rebellion against the authority of Her majesty the Queen, Empress of India;
>
> and whereas, during such rebellion, Her Majesty's Representative and other officers were murdered at Imphal on the 24th of March last;

and whereas by a Proclamation dated the 19th April 1891 the authority of the Regent, Kula Chandra Singh, was declared to be at an end,

and the administration of the State was assumed by the General Officer Commanding Her Majesty's forces in Manipur territory;

"Manipur State has become liable to the penalty of annexation, and is now at the disposal of the Crown;

and that "Her Majesty the Queen, Empress of India has been pleased to forego Her right to annex to Her Indian Dominions the territories of the Manipur State;

and has graciously assented to the re-establishment of Native State".

A notification was issued on 18th September, 1891 that:

"the Governor-General in Council has chosen Chura Chand son of Chowbi Yaima, and great grand son of Raja Nara Singh of Manipur to be Raja of Manipur."

A sanad was issued by the Secretary to the Government of India with the following statement

"The Governor-General in Council has been pleased to select you, Chura Chand, son of Chowbi Yaima, to be the Chief of the Manipur State;

and you are hereby granted the title of Raja of Manipur, and a salute of eleven guns.

"The Chiefship of the Manipur State and the title and salute will be hereditary in your family;

and will descend in the direct line by primogeniture, provided that in each case the succession is approved by the Government of India".

British Rule in Manipur

The policy of British Paramountcy in Manipur (1891-1947) had several aspects. The British declared their supremacy with the occupation of Manipur; British India became the paramount power. As a signal of British paramountcy, the British Indian Government declared that Manipur had committed a rebellion against Queen Empress so she had to pay penalty for this; the British disarmed the people, imposed a fine of Rs. 2,50,000 payable in five years; and an annual tribute of Rs. 50,000. She took the responsibility of the overall defence and security of the native State. As a first step, the Government of India converted the British Political Agency as the governing authority of Manipur. Earlier in the pre-colonial period, the Political Agent performed the ambassadorial functions with the authority to protect British interest in North-Eastern Frontier including Manipur. Government of India retained the 44th Gurkha Rifles of the Indian Army to defend Manipur. As a condition for the selection of a minor prince Churachand Singh, the British Indian Government took over the administration of Manipur during his minority. The British Indian Government introduced the British Indian administrative system in Manipur. The Political Agent was also the Superintendent of the State. There were twelve Political Agents in the pre-colonial period and fourteen Political Agents during the colonial period 1891-1947. The Political Agent was entrusted with the powers and function of a Judge-Magistrate, the Executive Head of administration and the Chief of the Police administration. He was overall in-charge of the administration of the hill tribes. The Political Agent was under the supervision of the Chief Commissioner of Assam. Moreover, the Political Agent was the representative of the British Crown.

Over and above the imposition of the fine and a tribute on the State, the British followed a policy of extracting resources of the State to meet the cost of the administration. They introduced a new taxation system under which they imposed house tax on the people: valley house tax and hill house tax. The rate of valley house tax was Rs. 2 per house and the hill house tax was Rs. 3 per house. The amount of tax was too heavy and people could not face the consequences of the monetization of their economy. The self sufficiency economy enjoyed by Manipur during the pre-colonial period had undergone a great change after 1891. British introduced a free trade system as a part of their colonial economic policy. They controlled the trade and industry in the State. They allowed the export of rice freely to Kohima and other military stations. They imported a large quantity of salt from outside; Liverpool salt was imported to Manipur through Burma as a result the salt industry in Manipur (manufacture of salt cakes from brine) was greatly affected. The import of Liverpool salt was to compete with the production of the brine wells of the State. The British also imported other commodities and ultimately led to the decline of the indigenous cottage industries.

Administration of Justice

The British colonial administration aimed to keep law and order, collect taxes to maintain the cost of administration and adjudicate disputes among the people. Therefore, the administration went in for the establishment of a police system, a revenue system and judicial administration. This three pronged policy brought a marked change in the administration under the British. Thus Major Maxwell, the Political Agent introduced a new system of administration of justice and police in 1892. He proclaimed, "Rules for the Administration of Justice and Police in the Manipur State - 1892."[6] A colonial policy implied the change in the judicial system. The Rules envisaged three branches of judicial administration; the Panchayat court, the Chirap Court and the Political Agent's Court.

The Chief Commissioner of Assam exercised supervisory judicial power on the courts of Manipur. He had revisional powers in all cases. He had to confirm criminal cases of death and imprisonment beyond 7 years. He had the right to call for the records in any case tried by the courts in Manipur and reverse the sentence if he deemed it fit.

This judicial system consolidated the British rule in Manipur and was continued up to 1947 when the Maharaja of Manipur passed two laws to deal with judicial matters; Manipur Courts Act, 1947 and Manipur Hill People Regulation, 1947.

Police Administration

The military force was a necessary condition for the consolidation of the Imperial power in a newly conquered territory. They needed a political security for the economic exploitation of the new territory for the development of colonial power. In Manipur, the question of political security was very crucial. The Government of India recognized the supreme strategic importance of the State. Manipur occupies a commanding position between Assam and Burma which required the location of a military base of the Indian Army. Manipur is also situated between the Naga Hills and Lushai Hills of Assam which were conquered by British recently. Therefore, it was decided to station a Military regiment in Manipur. Major Maxwell was reported to have commented, "Take away the British support, the country would be involved in a revolution tomorrow."[7] The need of the internal security of the State was reflected in the establishment of two wings of the police: the civil police and the military police.

Civil Police

The British Political Agent provided for the *Chowkidari* system in Manipur. A *chowkidar* was a rural police who was appointed to every hundred houses. His duty was to keep himself cognizant of what went on in his circle of villages without of course interfering into the domestic or private life of the people. He was subordinate to the panchayat of the circle. The chowkidar was elected by the people of the area subjcct to the confirmation of the Political Agent.

In course of time, a small civil police was started in January, 1893 for working in the urban areas. The British had created a territorial reserve known as the British Reserve Area within the town of Imphal consisting of the main Kangla Fort area and Khwairamband bazaar and nearby villages. The Briritish Reserve became centre of political and military power of the British rule in Manipur. The Political Agency and other branches of the administration including residences of the colonial officers and cantonment of the occupation army were located within the British Reserve.

Military Police

The Government established a military police of one battalion. One M.L.F. Crawford, the Assistant Political Agent was appointed the adjutant of Manipur State Police. The new military police force was armed with muzzle loading carbine and bayonet, and *dhoti* with brown leather accoutrement. They were trained by the instructors of Naga Hills military police. The number of sepoys in the military police consisted of many Manipuri local recruits and the number was reduced due to desertion in 1894. Later on Nepalese were recruited in place of the Manipuri.

When the administration was handed over to Raja Churachand Singh, he became the commandant of the Manipur State Police. The administration of the police was looked after by the police member of the Manipur State Durbar since 1907. The police member became an important functionary of the administration under the Raja. During the World War I the strength of the Manipur State police was increased. He continued to hold the charge of the commandant of the State military police up to 31st May 1941. And on 1st June 1941 E.E. Hughes was appointed the first Superintendent of Police Manipur. The post of the Superintendent of Police and Commandant of the Manipur Rifle in the beginning were combined in one person. Before the World War II an attempt was made to reorganize the Manipur State police but there was not much success. Later on after the independence, the Manipur State Government converted the Manipur State police to Manipur Rifles.[8]

Revenue Administration

Collection of taxes was a main function of a colonial government in order to finance the cost of administration. The British Government abolished the feudal system of Lallup and slavery in Manipur. These two steps were a great departure from the traditional system of administration.

Lallup was a feudal service rendered by the subjects of Manipur to the king in pre-colonial period. As a marked departure from the rule of the Meitei monarch, the British abolished the Lallup service. It was a sort of official abolition of the feudal service in Manipur.

Slavery existed in Manipur since the ancient times. But in the later part of the 19th century, in 1891 at the time of British conquest, the Manipur king had 1200 slaves maintained by the royal household. The nobles who were members of the bureaucracy had slaves in their households. The slavery system in Manipur was mild and human. The British policy was for the abolition of the slavery in England and in the colonies. So Major Maxwell, the Political Agent who did some exercise on the institution of Lallup and slavery announced the abolition of both Lallup and slavery on 29th April 1892. The abolition of Lallup was welcomed by the common people who suffered from this system. However, the abolition of slavery did not bring salvation to the slaves immediately. At the same time, it was not beneficial financially to the slaves.

In lieu of the Lallup service, every household in the valley of Manipur was to pay a house tax of Rs. 2 per annum. A revenue of Rs. 5 per hectare of land (locally known as *pari*) was to be paid. For the hill areas, a house tax of Rs. 3 per annum was imposed. The Government then decided to make a cadastral survey of the lands occupied in the valley of Manipur. The land was classified in to agricultural lands, homesteads and community lands used for grazing and other community purposes. It was a gigantic task for the new colonial administration to carry out survey of the land holdings and record the rights of the land owners in a document known as the *patta*. The revenue administration was carried out by the Political Agent with the help of his assistant Political Agents. Major Maxwell revived the pre-colonial divisions of the valley of Manipur in to four territorial districts known as *Panna*: *Ahallup Panna, Naharup Panna, Khabam Panna and Laipham Panna.* One official named *Lakpa* was appointed to each of the *Panna.* He was entrusted with the survey of the land which meant recording of the size, quality and type of land occupied by individuals. In actuality it was the adoption of the Indian pattern of revenue administration prevalent in Assam and Bengal. A *Lakpa* was assisted by petty official known as Amin, Konungo and peons. The *Lakpa* was not given salaries. He was to take 10% of the assessment of the revenue he made in his circle. The British Government expressed satisfaction at the initial success of the revenue administration.

This system increased the collection of revenues and it was continued till the year 1906. Major Maxwell sent out the *Lakpas* to different *Pannas* for the collection of revenue. The payment of 10% commission was abolished and salaries were paid to them. He also asked the village head men to collect arrear revenues from their respective villages. The new land revenue system was more or less successful.

Other sources of revenue were house tax, foreigner tax of Rs. 5 per annum per family, fishery, salt, forest, tea seeds, fines from law and justice and jail etc. The foreign residents had to pay a tax of 4 annas for grazing of their cattle. With the introduction of the hill house tax many nomadic Kuki villages were brought under permanent settlement and they paid house tax to the State. Next to the land tax, fisheries and salt industries provided revenue to the State. Maxwell of course abolished the State monopoly of trade in tea seeds. The forest in the initial stage did not produce any revenue to the State. However, the regulation of forestry in western hills near Jiribam was entrusted to the divisional forest officer, Cachar and collection of revenue was quite plenty.

A reference may be made to the economic policy of the British Government. Manipur did not have raw materials for the development of industries. The Maharajas of Manipur were opposed to the establishment of tea plantation in Manipur. The British Government did not attempt to encourage tea plantation. Once they tried to develop silk industry by involving a company from Calcutta. This plan was thought to be profitless and the proposal was dropped. The British rulers encouraged free trade towards Manipur. They encouraged external trade to be conducted by foreigners mostly those who belonged to the Marwari community. This community got favour both from the colonial authorities and Raja of Manipur. They monopolized the export of rice and import of manufactured goods. The British did not encourage industrialization.

The colonial Indian Government was influenced by certain social philosophy of the mother country. They implemented the utilitarian measures of welfare to the conquered people. The British in Manipur started with the establishment of schools both in the hills and valley of Manipur to produce petty government servants to be teachers, peons, *chowkidars*, amin and vaccinators. They provided minimum medical facilities through the establishment of dispensaries and hospitals. They were confronted with several deadly diseases like malaria, cholera and small pox which visited the State in epidemic forms. The colonial government constructed State roads.

The British Policy towards the Hill Tribes

After the British conquest of Manipur in 1891, the hill areas came under the rule of British Political Agent. The British introduced system of Indirect Rule over the hill tribes who were divided in to two major ethnic groups of the Nagas and the Kukis. Lord Lansdowne used a significant term "the Manipur people" to mean both the people of the valley and the hills. However, the Political Agent used the term 'Manipur' to mean Meiteis who dwell in the valley of Manipur.

Under the new system, the British did not rule the hill tribes directly. Like the pre-colonial rulers of Manipur they did not interfere in the affairs of the tribal villages. The *Lallup* system did not work in hill areas though the king imposed payment of tributes on the hill villages. Occasionally tribal villagers were sometimes used by the king for under taking public works; straightening of the course of rivers and digging of canals. Slavery existed among the tribes in a mild form. The British introduced the hill house tax of Rs. 3 per household per year. The chiefs or head men of the tribal villages were entrusted with the administration of their villages. The head man or the chief was to collect the hill house tax and submit to the State for which they got certain commission. In the beginning of the British rule there was no proper regulation for the administration of the hill tribes but the British Govvernment introduced the Chin Hills Regulation of 1896 to administer the hill tribes. It was quite effective. Therefore, the spirit of this regulation was adopted in Manipur as the guiding principle of hill administration.

Under the colonial system, the chief or head of the village was to collect house tax, maintain law and order and administer justice according to their customary laws. They were also made to render forced labour to the colonial authority for the construction and maintenance of bridle paths, roads and bridges. They also provided local hospitality to the touring officers, army, police and patty colonial employees. In practice, the *Lallup* system was de facto reimposed on the hill tribes in a more stringent form. These taxes produced anti colonial agitations.

The British laid down a policy that they were to look after the interest of the hill tribes and protect them from the operation of the administrators of the valley or the Raja. They had to act as a saviour or the protector of the hill tribes. The administration of the hill tribes was separated from that of the valley. This separation of administration on ethnic lines was greatly resented by the Raja of Manipur who was not allowed any intervention in the hill areas. Though the Political Agent was a colonial officer, the direct contact with the hill people was made by petty officials recruited from the people of the valley. For administration of the hill areas, the whole area was divided into five divisions known as Lam. The five *Lams* were in "the north the *Mao Lam*, and the *Tangkhul Lam* includes the hills along the north east of the valley, south of the Tangkhul country was the *Tammu Lam*; the *Moirang Lam* was in the south west corners of the State and the Kapui (Kabui) Lam to the west of the valley." Five *Lam* subedars for the five divisions. Under one Lam subedar, seven *Lambus* were appointed for a division. The *Lambu* in the pre-colonial Meitei monarchy was an important petty official for the rural areas. Under the colonial system, the *Lambu* was an interpreter, a process server and a peon combined in one. Its counterpart in the Naga hills was the *dobashi* or the interpreter. The *Lambu* was employed in all aspects of the colonial administration, keeping the law and order, administration of justice, supervision of public works. He was the ear and eye of the Government. During the period of British direct management of Manipur (1891-1906) the *Lambus* oppressed the people. The British rule ensured law and order; peace was maintained, taxes were collected, justice was administered. The hill people suffered greatly; they could not bear the financial burden of the house tax. The monetization of the economy by the introduction of the house tax was to the great hardship of the hill tribe who never experienced such suffering under the pre-colonial rule.

In 1907 when the administration was handed over to Raja Churachand Singh, The Political Agent continued to administer the hill tribes. The objective of the British policy was to prevent the traditional operation and exploitation of the hill tribes by the Raja and his government and to protect the hill tribe. They kept peace, prevented internal tribal feuds and warfare among the Nagas and Kukis and inter societal conflicts and imposed tax to meet the cost of administration. They maintained roads and bridges along the main roads from Imphal to neighbouring districts. The claim of the British which was to protect the tribal people was not translated in the ground level. In reality the British rule through the *Lambus* was oppressive.

In 1913, there was a reorganization of the State Durbar. The Raja ceased to be the President. One British ICS officer was appointed as the President. Not the Durbar but the President in his own discretion was entrusted to administer the hill area under the overall supervision of the Political Agent. In fact, the President of the Durbar popularly known as the PMSD, with his office at the capital town of Imphal was an overburdened officer of the State. He did not have officers to assist him. He could not go on tour in the hills. He depended on the *Lambus* and the *Lam subedars*. The

British imposed forced labour known as Potthang Begari and Potthang Senkhai. Very frequently, the tribal labour was subjected to physical torture. There were eighteen British PMSDs between 1913-1947. Among them were distinguished names like J.C. Higgins, Christopher Gimson, C.S. Mullan, Captain C.W.L. Harvey, G.P. Stewart and F.F. Pearson.

There were loopholes in the administration of the hill tribes. A great mistake was the absence of any clear-cut specific provision for the administration of hill areas under the Rules of management of State of Manipur which was introduced in 1907. This mistake was pointed out by Political Agent John Shakespeare himself. Between the hill men and the British officer, there intervened a most unsatisfactory intermediary in the form of Lambus who were responsible for dissatisfaction among the hill people. Sir Robert Reid, a Governor of Assam himself criticized the system when he observed:

> "there is no doubt that the administration had been seriously out of touch with heir hill subjects, that the latter were not always well treated, and that there were genuine grievances and genuine abuse."[9]

The Kuki Rebellion (1917-1919), described by colonial writers as 'the most serious incident in the history of Manipur and its relation with its hill subjects', led to a serious discussion on the future administration of the hills. The Chief Commissioner of Assam made a new pronouncement in October 1919 for the administration of hill areas.[10] It declared,

> "the good government of the hill tracts is an object in which Government of India are directly interested, . . . and approve the measures for the proper administration of the hills i.e., the opening of roads and bridle paths;
>
> the extension of education among the tribes;
>
> and the bringing of medical relief within the reach of the people of the hills".

The order also approved appointment of three sub-divisional officers of Assam Commission in three hill areas, one at North-west sub-division (Tamenglong), the second in Northeast sub-division (Ukhrul) and third at Southwest sub-division (Churachandpur).

The new Rules introduced in 1919 restated the relation between the Raja and the President of the Manipur State Durbar, "the hill tribes are administered on His Highness behalf by the President of the Durbar assisted by one or more Sub-Divisional Officer." The Rules laid down that His Highness's the Maharaja had a right to be consulted in all matters of importance concerning the hill tribes. The Manipur State Durbar exercised no direct control over the hills. But from time to time, it tried to claim some indirect control through its power over the budget. However, the officers who were to be appointed as SDOs were not easily available and the working of the sub divisions were not satisfactory due to the negligence and incompetence of the officers. The Government ultimately framed the Rules for the management of hill tribes in 1935 in which the revised rules announced in 1919 were incorporated. On the status of the administration of the hill areas, Secretary to the Governor of Assam made a pronouncement on 22nd April 1937. It said among others,

> "the most important sphere in which the Political Agent and the President of the Manipur State Durbar exercised control is over the hill tribes...from the installation of the present Maharaja, the hill tribes were treated as on a footing distinct from that of His Highness Manipuri subjects being only 'dependent on' the Manipur State. The phrase 'dependent on' exactly describes the position which has existed from time immemorial and still exist today. . ."

The pronouncement concluded

> ". . . History shows that the Manipuri cannot and will not give the hills an administration of the standard to which they are both entitled and accustomed and that it can only be maintained by the control now exercised. We are under an obligation to the hill tribes to maintain to them a decent administration. The consequences

of unrest and rebellion among them might be disastrous for Manipur and would be most dangerous for those portions of British India and Burma which lie along Manipur boundaries." [11]

First Women's Movement of 1904

The colonial economic policy brought financial difficulties on the inhabitants of the valley. It was thought that the abolition of Lallup would bring some relief in terms of freedom from forced labour. Political Agent Maxwell just after the war called up former members of the Manipur army and they were constituted into a labour corps. They were engaged in carrying supplies to the British forces on the Kohima road. They were also engaged in the maintenance of Imphal-Mao cart road. There was great resentment towards the employment of forced labour. As noted in the previous paragraph there was disaffection among the Rajkumars of the State. They were also not happy over the selection of the new Raja. They were also against the policy of disarming the population of the country. This was regarded as a policy of blatant oppression. The British imposed a fine on the State. The people were not used to payment of house taxes both in the valley and hill. The British Government introduced a new policy of export and import. Outwardly the British encouraged free trade in the State, however in reality they gave the monopoly of external or export trade to the few merchants from Marwar who were known as Marwaris or Kanias. The frustration of the people after 14 years of direct British rule bursted out in a movement which is popularly known in history of Manipur as first women's war. Some incidents preceded the outbreak. On 6th July, 1904 the Khwairamband market known as the Sanakeithel was burnt down; 28 market sheds which could accommodate 3,000 women vendors were destroyed and on 15th July, 1904 again the Bungalows of Captain Nuttal the tutor to the Raja Churachand Singh and Mr. Dunlop the Assistant Political Agent were destroyed by fire. There was also another fire in the night of 4th August, 1904, the authorities discovered a stick with an oil rag attached to it. Colonel Maxwell attributed the burning of this bungalow to the acts of incendiarism on the part of the

Manipuri inhabitants of the town instigated by the 'Rajkumars' or the descendents of the late ruling house as a symbol of their dislike for and a protest against the ruler who had been imposed on them. Maxwell as a Superintendent of the State issued an order to rebuild the bungalows of the British officials. He also asked the people of Imphal area to construct the bungalows with teak wood from the Kabaw valley of Burma. If the people declined he would threaten to impose punitive force on them.

The order of Superintendent Maxwell created a great consternation among the people. It was a temporary 'resuscitation' of *Lallup* on the urban people of Imphal. In the beginning the people did not have the courage to confront the order as they were demoralized by the impact of the war. On behalf of the people of Imphal areas an application was submitted to the Political Agent and the application was signed by one Chingsabam Natek Singh of Sagolband. It was rejected by Political Agent Maxwell. He entertained a prejudice against the Rajkumar families. He made derogatory remark on the Rajkumars. He wrote:

> "Rajkumar, very rarely works, his rank in most instances is sufficient inducement to the girls of the country to marry him and as he generally takes more wives than one and the women of Manipur are the bread winners of the family, he leads a life of indolence varied by grotesque acts of conceit in excess even of the attempt of the frog in the fable to expand herself in to the size of an ox. . . ."[12]

A protest meeting was convened for all the people of Imphal. The Superintendent imposed that assembly of more than five persons was unlawful and such a public meeting if held he would employ troops to disperse the meeting. Despite the strict warning of the authority a big meeting was organized on 30th September 1904 near the Cheirap Court. A big crowd of 5000 attended the meeting. The authorities disbursed the assembly and arrested six leaders who were presumed to be the leaders of the movement. They happened to be Rajkumars. A court of enquiry was constituted to try the arrested persons from 4th November, 1904 onwards.

Political Agent Maxwell on 10th November 1904 sentenced the culprits for expulsion from Manipur.

The women folk of the State were shocked at the punishment of the six Rajkumars. The market women came out spontaneously and organized a big demonstration. They marched to the Residency and protested against the Political Agent's action. The movement continued for several days resulting in tothe closure of the markets affecting day to-day life of the people. The movement was led by the market women leaders.The movement was against the reintroduction of *lallup* which was already abolished by the Government of India. It was a wrong step taken by Political Agent. The order for reconstruction was withdrawn. Chief Commissioner J.B. Fuller expressed unhappiness over this incident arising out of action of Political Agent. Political Agent Maxwell was transferred from the Political Agency.[13]

Christian Missions in Manipur

An objective of the British India was for 'civilizing the Asiatics' meaning the backward Indians. This mission was well expressed in the famous phrase of Rudyard Kipling, 'White men's burden' to civilize the conquered people. An instrument of the civilizing mission was Christian proselytism. There was a symbiotic relation between colonial rule and the Christian mission. The colonial ruler utilized the services of the missionaries in the field of education, medical and social reforms to spread the colonial rule among the Indian population. The first attempt to establish Christian mission in Manipur was under taken as early as 1836 by the American Baptist Mission in Burma.[14] The mission failed.

After 1891, a condition was laid down by the British authorities that they would not interfere in to the traditional polity system, religious belief and cultural practices of the people. Political Agent Major H. Maxwell wanted to follow this policy of non interference in to the social and religious life of the Hindu Meiteis of the Manipur valley and so discouraged Christian mission activities among the Hindu Meiteis who regarded Christianity as a religion of the conquering white men. The first initiative for a Christian mission work in Manipur was taken up by one Robert Arthington, a millionaire of Leeds in England. He established the Arthington Aboriginese Mission Society. His aim was of a mobile missionary movement. Even before the founding of the mission society, on 15th September, 1885 he wrote to the Assam Baptist Mission stating his desire to open a mission among the tribes. Arthington's interest towards Assam was aroused by one missionary named John Dalmas who was a missionary in Assam. The Arthington Mission Society appointed young William Pettigrew to start Christian evangelism in the State of Manipur among the Meiteis. Pettigrew came to India in 1891 but the political instability as a result of the Anglo-Manipur war of 1891; he had to wait four years for permission to enter Manipur. Meanwhile he started learning Bengali and Manipuri language. In 1894 William Pettigrew approached A. Porteous the acting Political Agent in Manipur for the permission. In the absence of Political Agent Maxwell the permission was granted by A. Porteous and William Pettigrew started work on 6th February, 1894 at Imphal. Pettigrew started to preach the gospel among them. Meanwhile Major Maxwell the Political Agent returned from his furlough and took an alarming view of the mission work and expressed his fear that trouble might arise in a protest from the Hindu Meiteis. Political Agent Maxwell knew the injunction made by the British Government of non-interference and strict neutrality in matters of religion. So Maxwell decided to maintain the status quo and serve the ultimatum that Pettigrew leave Imphal or stop his missionary work.

William Pettigrew was disappointed but Maxwell came to his rescue that he might work among the Tangkhul Nagas of north eastern hills of Manipur. Pettigrew established his mission at Ukhrul. He acted both as a missionary and unofficial State officer in the administration of the area. He kept close contact width the State officials at the capital. When Pettigrew was almost settled down he was recalled by the Arthington Society as he had completed three years. Pettigrew was not willing to return home and he applied to the American Baptist Missionary Union in Assam for help. In 1895 the Baptist Missionary Conference in Sibsagar seriously discussed the request of William Pettigrew. Accordingly Pettigrew was ordained as a missionary by the Sibsagar Baptist Church Assam which was endorsed by the executive committee of the American Baptist Mission in Boston in January, 1896.

William Pettigrew continued his work among the Tangkhul Nagas with great enthusiasm. The Government of Manipur did not allow the entry of more than one missionary in to the State. It appears from the report of William Pettigrew that the earlier years were dull and unpromising. However, he engaged himself in the construction of a mission bungalow, a school and study of local dialect i.e., Tangkhul and doing translation works. He hardly achieved anything substantial. He became quite conversant with the local dialects. He knew already Manipuri, he learned Tangkhul and Thadou. He asked his mission authorities to send another missionary to help him. But there was no response. During the visit of Viceroy, Lord Curzon to Manipur, he approached him to liberalize the policy on the number of missionary in Manipur. After the installation of Raja Churachand Singh and his Manipur State Durbar, Pettigrew renewed his request to the government. But the Manipur State Durbar rejected his plea. However Raja Churachand Singh was not hostile towards the missionary and advised that there should be no obstacle to the missionary work among the hill people on the condition that they should not make an attempt to spread their work in the valley of Manipur.

Political Agent John Shakespeare supported William Pettigrew. He was appointed as Superintendent of the census of Manipur Hill Tribes in 1910 -11 because he was the only man who knew the dialects known to the hill tribes. Pettigrew did the census work successfully with the help of his school teachers and his senior students. Unfortunately it made him a suspect that he was a subordinate official of the State. Here we see the combination of the mission and colonial authority.

Another missionary U.M. Fox was sent to Ukhrul in 1911 and Pettigrew left for England on leave in 1912. Meanwhile the students of Pettigrew who were educated at the Ukhrul Mission School became of age. Both Naga and Kuki students were employed in mission work. We may mention the contribution of M.K. Miksha and T. Luikham among the Naga students. Through the efforts of Kuki converts particularly Lungkhovel Kom and Teba Kilong. Christianity was spread among the western hills. The local churches grew up in a large number. And the Manipur Christian Association was formed in 1917. The first convention of this association was held in Ukhrul in 1917. This period coincided with last two years of the World War I in which the Kukis revolted. The mission activities were greatly affected and suspended for some time. The mission station was shifted to Kohima and William Pettigrew moved to Gauhati.

During the Kuki Rebellion, J.H. Higgins President of the Manipur State Durbar organized a tribal labour corps for service in France. William Pettigrew was called out from Gauhati and helped organize the labour corps consisting of 2000 men of whom 1200 were from the Tangkhuls. After the war, in recognition of the contribution made by the missionaries and Christian workers, the government of Manipur granted a land for the new mission headquarters at Kangpokpi.

Watkin Roberts, the Welsh Missionary

History records that a missionary named Watkin Roberts from Mizo hills visited a Hmar village named Senvawn in response to the invitation of the chief of the village (Kamkholun). Watkin Roberts recruited native workers among the Christian converts and established Thadou-Kuki Pioneer Mission with head quarters at Senvawn. William Pettigrew was perhaps not happy with the establishment of new mission in South Manipur with head quarter at Senvawn.

Now the rivalry between American Baptist and Welsh Presbyterian were indulging in the mission politics. William

Pettigrew who was a class mate of Political Agent Higgins tried to restrain the Presbyterian mission workers to enter Manipur. H.J. Higgins banned the entry of Presbyterian into Manipur. Meanwhile, Watkin Roberts changed the name of mission to North East India General Mission (NEIGM) in 1919. Unluckily Watkin Roberts was ousted from the NEIGM. He started a new mission called Indo-Burma Pioneer Mission. Therefore the supporters of Roberts's new mission formed the Independent Church in April 1930. Political Agent Higgins issued an order on 22nd November, 1930 prohibiting the Independent Church from holding any assembly or conference. After eleven years, Sir Robert Reid the Governor of Assam intervened on behalf of supporters of Watkin Roberts and Political agent C. Gimson on 11th April 1931 permitted the Independent Church to work in South Manipur.

Though the Manipur State Durbar did not permit Christian missionary work, the individual Christian families lived in the urban areas. The first Meitei Christian convert was A. Porom Singh, a student of William Pettigrew. However S.N. Parratt claimed that a Manipuri lady named Kaboklei related to the royalty was the first convert in Sylhet. The missionaries converted some individual tribals who lived in British Reserve Area at Imphal. However, in the colonial period, Christian missionary activities were not wide spread however it grew up at large scale in the post colonial period.

The Christian missions devoted to the establishment of primary schools; they published books mostly the *Bible* and other Biblical tracts, extended medical facilities, established churches in the villages and organized Christian solidarity organizations for the respective denominations and area wise associations. A Christian fraternity among the hill tribe was created. With the spread of western education the world view of the tribal was widened. They participated in the administration of the State. The colonial administrator as indicated by their involvement of the Christian missionaries in the State activities unwittingly showed the collusion between Christian mission and colonialism.

Rule of Raja Churachand Singh (1907-1941): The Manipur State Durbar

Selection of Churachand Singh as the Raja of Manipur by the British authorities was not welcomed by the people of Manipur. Churachand Singh was the son of Rajkumar Chaubi Yaima Singh who was a victim of prosecution by the past ruling house and Chaubi Yaima's family were almost forgotten. Prince Chaubi Yaima was involved in the rebellion of Prince Bora Chaoba. The rebellion failed; he fled to Cachar and died in 1887 at the village of Lalang. Churachand Singh, a minor of five years at the time of selection as the Raja of Manipur was born on 14th April, 1885. As mentioned above after several consultations in which Political Agent Major Maxwell played a decisive role Churachand Singh was selected as a Raja. The following genealogical tree prepared by Major Maxwell and other astrologers showed his claim to the throne of Manipur ruled by Ningthouja dynasty:

The genealogical tree of Raja Churachand Singh (1885-1941)

Garibniwaz (1709-1748)

Ngoubram Shai (Senapati) 11th Son

↓

Bhadra Singh (1825 King of Manipur during 7 years devastation)

Nara Singh (Regent and Maharaja of Manipur) (1833-1850)

Bhogendra Singh alias Bhubon

Chaubi Yaima (Sanayaima)

Four sons: Dumbra Singh, Dimb Singh, Chandrahas Singh and Churachand Singh (selected as the Raja)

The family of Churachand Singh was very poor. His father did not leave behind anything for the family. Chaubi Yaima left behind two wives, Lalitamanjuri and Nitrapati. Luckily his mother Lalitmanjuri was the daughter of a leading noble of Moirang. He acted as a guardian of the sons and daughters of the two wives of Chaubi Yaima Singh.

Raja Churachand Singh was a child of destiny. After his selection as the Raja, the Political Agent provided enough funds for the maintenance of the Raja and his family of two mothers and eight children. The maternal grand father of Churachand Singh, Moirangthem Ramananda Singh was appointed as the *Moirang Ningthou,* Chief of Moirang by the Political Agent. The investiture of Churachand as the Raja of Manipur was performed on 29th April, 1892 in a grand function at the Polo Ground of the capital where the Political Agent Major Maxwell read out Sanad of the Government of India appointing him as the Raja of Manipur. During his minority, the Government of India appointed Major Maxwell as the Superintendent of the State of Manipur.

The British Government of India made arrangement for the education of Raja Churachand Singh and his half brother Rajkumar Digendra Singh in Mayo College, Ajmer. This college was meant only for the royal princes of the princely States of India. The British intention was to train up Raja Churachand Singh as a ruler loyal to the British. Raja Churachand Singh was educated in Mayo College for 6 years (1885-1901). He was tolerably good in studies and was interested in sports; polo, hockey, football and cricket. While in Ajmer Churachand Singh came to know of other Rajput princes of the time. He received the medals awarded by several rulers of Rajputana.

After the completion of his education at Mayo College, Captain J.R. Nuttall of 44th Gurkha Rifles was appointed tutor to the Raja for 5 years till he came of age. In 1901 the Government of India established the Imperial Cadet Corps (ICC) at Dehra Dun to give military training to the princes of native States. Churachand Singh also joined the corps. He got training in warfare. Churachand Singh came out to Manipur in 1907. During his education days he used to have consultations with the Political Agents on the administration of Manipur.

Lord Curzon and Churachand Singh (1901)

In 1901 Lord Curzon, the British Viceroy visited Manipur. Churachand Singh as a minor did not participate in the administration. In a special Durbar, the British Political Agent introduced Raja Churachand Singh to Lord Curzon who gave a public reception to the young Raja.

Manipur was under the direct British rule for 16 years (1891-1906). It was the period of minority of Raja Churachand. At the age of 22, Raja Churachand Singh was handed over the administration of the State of Manipur by Sir Lancelot Haire, the Lieutenant Governor of Eastern Bengal and Assam on 15th May 1907. However, the administration of the hill areas was not entrusted to him. The Political Agent controlled the hills. A new Rule for the Management of Manipur State was announced. According to this law the Manipur State Durbar was created.

The Raja as the President of the Manipur State Durbar

Raja Churachand Singh was the President of the Manipur State Durbar. The Vice President was the Assistant Political Agent who belonged to the Indian Civil Service. There were other six members divided in to two categories; ordinary member and additional member. The Manipur State Durbar was a Council of ministers appointed by the British Government on the recommendation of the Raja and the Political Agent. Five members were appointed as the members of the first Durbar.

The Raja was responsible for the administration of the valley of Manipur. He was assisted by the Durbar. The decisions of the Durbar were to be approved by the Raja with the copies submitted to the Political Agent. The members of the Durbar acted de facto as ministers of the Raja. The Durbar also acted as a highest original and appellate court both civil and criminal. It could pass sentences including death, subject to confirmation by the Raja in the case of imprisonment of 5 years and above and by the Governor in case of death. The Raja had the powers of pardon in criminal cases and revisionary powers in both civil and criminal cases subject to the approval of the Political Agent.

In 1916 when the Raja vacated the position of the President of the Durbar, the PMSD or the President of the Manipur State Durbar looked after the administration of both the hills and valley. The PMSD looked after the fiscal administration of the State and prepared budget of the State. The Manipur State Durbar attracted a large number of educated Manipuris. It provided an administrative forum in which the educated persons could get political appointments and through them the State could get legitimacy or support of the people.

The Maharaja and the British Government

The British policy was that by education and training the new ruler of Manipur would appreciate their custom, language and traditional polity with full knowledge of the princely States of India and trust in the British Empire. Churachand Singh extended help to the British which confirmed the trust reposed on him. The Manipur Raja gave help to the British while dealing with the Abor Expedition in Eastern Himalayas (1911) and troubles in Sadiya. During the World War I (1914 -1919) Manipur Maharaja extended help to the British in form of Double Company of Manipuri soldiers, 2000 labour, ambulance and a war plane.

During the World War I the Kukis of Manipur revolted against the British and the King. It took one and half years of intensive military operation by the joint forces of Burma Military Police and Assam Rifles to suppress the Kuki rebellion (1917-1919). Raja Churachand Singh again extended the help to the British. The king himself participated in the operation against Dampi Kuki village for which he was given title of 'Dampi Ngamba'(conqueror of Dampi). The British were satisfied and announced the following relief for Manipur. They reduced the amount of tribute; three hill sub divisions were created; the Imphal-Mao road was to be constructed by the British; and Raja Churachand Singh was given the title of Maharaja instead of Raja and C.B.E awarded to him. The other anti colonial movements before the outbreak of the Kuki Rebellion were a series of agitations for the abolition of pothang (force) labour and other obnoxious practices introduced by the Manipur State Durbar in the valley. After the Kuki Rebellion, there was the Naga Raj Movement led by Jadonang and Gaidinliu in the western hills of Manipur. Jadonang was executed and Gaidinliu was imprisoned for life by the British. The movement continued for several years in western hills of Manipur, southern Naga Hills and north Cachar hills.

Award of K.C.S.I (1934)

Viceroy Lord Irwin accompanied by Lady Irwin and his daughter Miss Anneewood visited Manipur. He was given a great reception by the Maharaja of Manipur. Lord Irwin was an intelligent British statesman. He described the State of Manipur as the 'Switzerland of the east'. In 1934 the Maharaja was awarded the title of K.C.S.I. (Knight Commander of the Star of India). It was the climax of Maharaja Churachand's rule.

Maharaja Churachand Singh was a patron of modern education and western sports in Manipur. He encouraged establishment of schools and provided scholarships to the bright Manipur students for education outside the State. They were educated at Gauhati, Sylhet, Dacca, Calcutta and Benaras. He regarded himself as a patron of Vaishnavism in Manipur. He presided over the Brahma Sabha consisting of many learned Brahmin scholars who were conversant with Hindu scriptures. He also tried to unite the Manipuris into a pan Manipuri forum known as Akhil Manipuri Hindu Maha Sabha to deal with the Manipuri national question. He also built up a fraternal relation with the hill tribes particularly, the Kabuis, the Tangkhuls and Kukis.

Difference between the Maharaja and the Colonial authorities

In his last days, the Maharaja faced troubles with the rising elite leadership. He fell out with the Nikhil Manipuri Maha Sabha. He utilized the services of the conservative and orthodox Brahma Sabha to collect religious fines on Hindu out castes. He had to deal with the women agitation of 1939 which was originally an agitation of market women against the policy of rice exports monopolized by the Marwari community which was converted to a demand for political reforms. The British were against introduction of democratic system in Manipur.

The greatest political upheaval faced by Maharaja Churachand Singh and British colonial authorities was this women agitation. The market women of Manipur initiated the protest movement which lasted 15 months. This protest movement is known in the history of Manipur as the 'Great Second Women Agitation of Manipur' popularly known as '*Nupi Lan*' (Women's War, 1939-40). It was an anti feudal, anti monopoly and anti colonial movement. The women agitation succeeded in banning the export of rice to outside Manipur but due to the intervention of Nikhil Manipuri Mahasabha particularly its popular leader Hijam Irabot Singh, it was converted into a movement for democratic reform. The agitation died down after the imprisonment of Irabot Singh in 1940 and outbreak of World War II which stopped all talks about constitutional reforms in Manipur.

The ailing Maharaja Sir Churachand Singh thought of abdicating the throne; he spent his last days in Nabadwip in Bengal. And his son Jubraj Bodhchandra Singh was appointed the succeeding Maharaja of Manipur in 1941. Maharaja Churachand Singh extended help to the British in the early years of the World War II but he could not do much due to his death at the age of 55 on 6th November, 1941. His son Maharaja Bodhchandra Singh extended the needed help to the British and the allied powers during the great battle of Imphal of 1944. Maharaja Bodh Chandra's assistance to the British was acknowledged by King Emperor

George VI by the exemption of the annual tribute of Rs. 50,000 payable to the British Empire. The British government also extended relief measures for the reconstruction of Manipur State. The British understood that there were political movements launched by different political parties particularly, the Manipur State Congress and Manipur Krishak Sabha for the introduction of responsible government in the State. Maharaja Bodh Chandra Singh who was a member of the Chamber of Indian Princes was advised by Viceroy, Lord Mountbatten and fellow princes to join the Dominion of India in the eventual declaration of Independence of India. Advised by the Chamber of Princes, Maharaja Bodh Chandra signed two significant agreements namely, the Stand Still Agreement and the Instrument of Accession on 11th August, 1947. Thus 4 days before the declaration of Independence of India, the Maharaja acceded the State of Manipur to the Dominion of India according to which he agreed to hand over subjects of defence, external affairs , finance including coinage and currency and communication. After the war, the British supported the Maharaja for the introduction of a constitutional monarchy in the State. The Maharaja promulgated two important laws for the State; the Manipur State Constitution Act 1947 and the Manipur Hill People Regulation 1947. Power was transferred by the British to the Maharaja Bodh Chandra Singh on 15th August, 1947.

The British rule in Manipur lasted for 56 years; the policy they desired was put in to practice in the first phase of their rule. Their Indirect Rule both in the valley and in the hills was fraught with troubles. They brought British liberal ideas, European technology and western education which formed the basis of modernization of Manipur.

FOOTNOTES

1. The formulation is based on Gangmumei Kamei's, "Colonialism and Colonial Policy" in Ethnicity and Social Change (An Anthology of Essays) New Delhi, 2008.

2. Hurd, John II was an American Professor of Oakland University. He wrote 'the Economic Consequences of Indirect Rule in India' which was published in the Indian Economic and Social History Review, 1975 Vol.2.

3. *Ibid.*

4. Mrs Grimwoods's book, "My Three Years in Manipur" and Mano Mohan Ghose's "Did Manipuri Princes obtain a fair trial?" published in the same year 1891, further publicized the action of Government of India and the injustice of their policy.

5. The history of British Rule in Manipur is widely discussed by British historians in the colonial period; John Shakespeare's, Manipur under direct British management (1907) and Robert Reid's History of Areas bordering Assam (Chapter on Manipur), 1942. B.C. Allen *District Gazetter of Naga Hills and Manipur* (1905).

6. Reproduced in Kh. Sarojini Devi, Political Agency in Manipur 1835-1947, 2005, Imphal pp. 116-124 as Appendix X, Administrative Report of Manipur Political Agency 1892-93, Shillong, and John Shakespeare, Manipur under British Management 1891-1907, Shillong, 1907.

7. Dena, Lal, Anomalies of the British colonial policy towards Manipur in the Modern History of Manipur, 1991, Imphal

8. Devi, Kh. Sarojini, *op cit,* pp. 116; N. Joykumar Singh, *Colonialism to Democracy: A History of Manipur 1819 to 1972,* pp. 100-105; L. Gopal Singh, *A History of Manipur Police*, 1986, Imphal.

9. Shakespeare, John, *op cit* pp. 3, N. Joykumar Singh, *op cit,* pp. 104

10. Allen, B.C. 1905, *Gazetteer of Naga Hills and Manipur*, Reprinted by Mittal Publications, New Delhi in 2002, pp.120.

11. Reid, Sir Robert, *History of the Frontier Areas Bordering on Assam from 1883-1941,* Shillong 1942 pp. 79

12. Order No. D of the Political Agency Manipur, dated 20th September 1904 quoted in N. Joykumar Singh opcit pp. 115.

13. Devi, M.K. Binodini, *Bora Saab Ongbi Sanatombi was a historical novel dealing with the romantic life of Colonel Maxwell and princess Sanatombi daughter of ex-Maharaja Surchandra Singh.*

14. Sword, V.H. *Baptist in Assam: A century of Missionary Service, 1836-1936*, Illinois 1935 pp.116 quoted in Lal Dena's Christian Missions and Colonialism, 1988, Shillong.

REFERENCES

Administrative reports of Manipur from 1891-1946.

Dena, Lal. *Christian Missions and Colonialism*, Shillong, 1986.

Downs, F.S. *The Mighty Works of God*, Gauhati, 1980.

Evans, E.W. (Ed), *Methods and Principles of Colonial Administration*, London, 1950.

Furnivall, F.S. *Colonial Policy and Practice*, London, 1948.

Kamei, Gangmumei, *Rajkumar Sanahal Singh*, B.Com, Memorial Lecture, Maharaj Sir Churachand Singh (1891-1941) in Modern Period of Manipur History, organised by Manipuri Sahitya Parishad, Imphal, 2006

Lal Dena (ed), *William Pettigrew: A Centenary Tribute*, Published by Ashok Tipnis, Imphal, 1996

Luikham, T. *A short history of Manipur Baptist Christian*, Calcutta, 1948.

Misra, B.B. *Administrative History of India 1834-1947*, Oxford University Press, New Delhi, 1970.

Neill, Stephen, *Colonialism and Christian Mission*, London, 1966.

Ningthougi chahi yangkhei subagi wari (Story of fifty years of the King) published on the occasion of Golden Jubilee celebration of Maharaj Sir Churachand Singh, Imphal, 1941.

Parratt explained the British rule in Manipur as a combination of British colonialism, feudalism of Raja Churachand Singh and Brahminism of Manipuri Hindus.

Parratt, John, *The Wounded Land: Politics and Identity in Modern Manipur*, New Delhi, 2005.

Pettigrew, William, *Twentyfive Years. 1897-1922*, Ukhrul Mission School, 1922.

Raunier, Rene, *Sociology of Colonies*, Vol.I, Routledge and Kegan Paul, London, 1948.

Resolutions of the Manipur State Durbar (1907-1946).

Roy, Singh, *History of Manipur*, Calcutta 1958.

Singh, K. Manimohan, *Christian Missionary Movement in Manipur*, Imphal, 1990.

Singh, N. Joykumar, *Colonialism to Democracy: A History of Manipur from 1819-1972*, 2002.

Singh, N. Lokendra *Unquiet Valley*, 1998.

Singh, R.K. Jhalajit, *A Short History of Manipur*, Imphal, 1965.

Singh, R.K. Sanahal, *Manipur Itihas*, Imphal 1947.

Stranse-Hupe and Harry W. Hozard, *Ideas of Colonialism*, New York, 1958.

4

The Ethno-Nationalism in Manipur

I

ETHNO-NATIONALISM

The *Harvard Encyclopedia of Ethnic Groups* (1980) explains that the word 'ethnic' derives via Latin from the Greek *ethnikos*, the adjectival form of *ethnos*, a nation or race. As originally used in English, ethnic signified "not Christian or Jewish, pagan, heathen"; for example, in the *Leviathan* Thomas Hobbes exhorted Christian converts to continue obeying their "ethnic" rulers. "Nation" comes from Latin via French; its ultimate source is *nasci*, "to be born," and the closer source is *nation*, meaning originally "birth", later one of the barbarian tribes outside the Roman world.[1]

Ethno-nationalism is a term used by Walker Connor, an American political scientist who wrote extensively on this concept which is an aspect of nationalism.[2] The term ethno-nationalism has come to be associated with Walker Connor. Etymologically, the term ethno-nationalism is a compound of two terms namely ethno and nationalism. Ethno is a Greek word meaning people and nationalism means the sense of loyalty and devotion to the ethnic group to which the individual or the group belongs. Walker Connor himself explains, "What is ethnonationalism and how does it differ from just plain nationalism? The answer is that there is no difference if nationalism is used in its proper sense."[3] He defines the nation and nationalism, "Nation connotes a group of people who believe they are ancestrally related. Nationalism connotes identification with and loyalty to one's nation as just defined. It does not refer to loyalty to one's country."[4] Walker Connor prefers the term ethno-nationalism to explain the phenomenon.

Daniele Conversi emphasizes the enduring power of the emotional depth of ethno national identity. He observes that the term denotes both the loyalty to an ethnic group embodied in a specific State, particularly where the latter is conceived as a nation State.[5] Walker Connor again explains

> "The two loyalties represent two very different order of things. Loyalty to State is socio-political in nature, and is based in large part on national self interest. Loyalty to nation is more intuitive than rational, and is predicated upon a sense of consanguinity – common ancestry. When the two are viewed as being in irreconcilable conflict, loyalty to the nation customarily proves the more powerful."

He further observes

> "the term ethno-nationalism therefore contains an inner redundancy. If nationalism were consistently employed to refer to the nation or ethnos, then ethno-nationalism would be a one-word tautology (i.e., "national nationalism.")

It is used simply to make certain that others are aware that what is being referred to is not loyalty to the State but loyalty to the extended family."[6] It denotes 'both the loyalty to a nation deprived of its own State and the loyalty to the ethnic group embodied in a specific State.' Ethno-nationalism tries to restore the ethnic connotation to nationalism as Connor believes that all forms of nationalism have an ethnic core.

Anthony D. Smith observes that since the 18th century there has been a revival of ethnicity in the national movement. He also concurs with the phenomenon of ethno-nationalism as explained by Walker Connor as a modernized form of nationalism.[7]

Sanjib Baruah's *Ethnonationalism in India* examines both the theory and practice of ethno-nationalism in this vast country.

According to him, "Ethnonationalism is a term that refers to a wide range of political phenomena including what may be called nationalism, separatism, secessionism, sub-nationalism, ethnic insurgency, ethnic militancy, or sometimes simply regionalism. It is best thought of as 'a heterogeneous set of "nation"-oriented idioms, practices, and possibilities that are continuously available or "endemic" in modern cultural and political life.'[8] He classifies the Indian ethnonationalism movements into three categories, (a) conflicts old and new that involve ethnonationalism mobilization, (b) elements of ethnonationaliam representation in the structure of Indian federalism and power sharing in Indian polity and (c) politics of India's diversity: multiplicity of languages, religions, castes and tribes.[9]

In the context of Manipur, there are three movements of ethno-nationalism, the Meitei nationalist movement, the fall out of Naga national movement on Manipur and the Kuki problem. We propose to explain these three movements in the conceptual framework of ethno-nationalism. Ethnicity is a major factor in the political movements of Manipur. The ethnic movements in Manipur may be taken as an example of politicization of ethnicity. And Joseph Rothschild describes this as an instance of politicized ethnicity assertiveness.[10]

II

Ethno Nationalism of the Meiteis

Manipur was an ancient kingdom. Her pre-Hindu names, Kangleipak or Meitrabak indicate that it was essentially a nation State of the Meiteis. The military expansion of the Meitei State to the surrounding hills and the conquest of Kabaw valley in Upper Burma in 1471 made the kingdom a multiethnic State dominated by the Meiteis and their monarchs. Since the transfer of the coveted Kabaw valley to Burma in 1834, Manipur's territory was reduced to the present geographical boundaries. It has become a trio ethnic State of the Meiteis, Nagas and Kukis, dominated by the Meiteis. The repeated wars and conquests against the neighbouring kingdoms particularly Burma which tried to eliminate the Meitei State and nation aroused a strong feeling of nationalism among the Meiteis. The Meitei nationalism is the sense of loyalty and devotion to both the Meitei ethnic group (Meitei nationality) and the Meitei State. The British conquered Manipur in 1891; she lost her independence and was reduced to a princely State under the British paramountcy. In 1949, the united Manipur was merged with India. The denial of democratic constitutional rights to the people of Manipur aroused the Meitei nationalism again during the post colonial period. There grew up several movements, resorting to arms struggle for national liberation of the people of Manipur from the republic of India. The merger of the State of Manipur to India was a controversial landmark in the modern history of Manipur. India is a plural society and a multiethnic State. Indian nationalism which tries to accommodate the Meitei identity cannot harmonise the Meitei nationalism.

Several writers have commented on the nature of these movements whether they be called insurgency or revolutionary movements. The Government of India used several terms to describe the ethnic movements by using disparaging terms like hostiles or underground. Insurgents are those who indulge in insurgency which means armed opposition to the established authority of the government. It is used in the sense of a rebel who is not yet recognized as a belligerent. It is a term used by the establishment towards those who oppose the State. Historically, insurgency was used in the sense of rebellion. A closer look to the movements in the North East shows that ethnic movements aim at the liberation of the ethnic groups in which they use armed struggle. Therefore ethnic insurgency is not a term empathetic to the movements. It was also raised by some writers that the term revolution should be used to describe the armed movements in Manipur. Saroj Nalini Parratt and Naorem Sanajaoba used the term insurgent or insurgency to describe the ethno national movements in Manipur.[11] N. Joykumar Singh prefers to describe these movements as revolutionary movements.[12] Gangmumei Kamei describes this deep rooted assertion of the ethnic nationalism as revolutionary.[13] It is a clear case of ethnonationalism of the Meiteis. Since ethnicity has been the core of the revolution, sociologically it may be described as a phenomenon of 'publicized ethnicity assertiveness of the Meiteis'.

What Lenin wrote is relevant

> "revolution is a change which breaks the old order to its new foundation, a drastic change of an existing social system, to achieve the objectives of a revolution by a destruction of the old and creation of a new society and consolidation of a new social relation."[14]

This description of a revolution fits into the revolutionary movement in Manipur during the post colonial period. These revolutionary movements are mostly nationalist in nature and popularly regarded as the national liberation movements.

There are several classifications of revolution. Of these the following may be regarded as being relevant to Manipur. During the pre colonial period, palace revolution due to struggle for power among the princes was most popular; insurrections against the king or the State are popular throughout the colonial period of history. A national revolution in a small scale was often attempted by the revolutionaries. Almost every armed movement is based on guerilla warfare.

The narrative of the movements may be preceded by an analysis of the forces which led to the outbreak of the revolutionary movements. Every event had cause and effect. A historical explanation of the political phenomena is given herewith.

The Rise of the Meitei Nationalism

The revolutionary movements in Manipur are an outcome of several deep rooted factors, namely the crisis of identity which was the motivating factor in the revival of Meitei nationalism, Indian apathy towards the political aspirations of the people of Manipur after the merger with India, economic exploitation and the policy of internal economy followed towards Manipur, the bureaucratic corruption as a result of the imposition of central rule in Manipur for 23 years (1949-1972), growth of highly educated elite group followed by a serious problem of unemployment of the youths, exposure of the discontented leaders to the ideas of revolution in many countries of the third world including Marxist ideas.

Regarding the crisis of identity or fear of losing it, the author wrote,

> "The myth of Aryan origin of the Meitei, which was created by the Brahmanical scholars after their conversion into Hinduism in the 18th century has now been exploded. The confusion between race, language, culture and Hindu religion led the people to think that their profession of Hinduism made them Aryans. The Meiteis are racially and linguistically Tibeto-Burmans with Tai and some Aryan admixtures due to immigration from different regions in different periods of history. The myth of Aryan connection which provided a strong base for belonging to Hindu world of India was questioned first by the Sanamahi cult, the pre-Hindu Meitei religion. This move was in the early stage against the Brahmin exploitation and advocated the preservation and promotion of the racial and cultural identity of the Meitei.
>
> "The Sanamahi cult revived the Meitei script, old literature and contributed greatly to the reassertion of the distinct Meitei identity. This movement turns out to be at later stage anti-Hindu and to some extent anti outsider. This assertion of identity in political system means sovereignty of Manipur, the Meitei cultural tradition and separateness of Manipur from the rest of India...The Meitei nationalism has been simultaneously aroused...It is strongly felt that the Meitei identity can be preserved and fostered in a Meitei sovereign State...The fear of being swallowed up by the great Indian multitude due to the influx of immigrants from outside causing immense demographic imbalance and thus causing the loss of cultural identity of the people is strongly felt. The intense search for self identity...is the greatest motivating factor in the revival of Meitei nationalism.[15]"

As nationalism means loyalty and devotion to the ethnic group and State, the Meitei nationalism means loyalty to the Meitei as a nationality and loyalty to the multi ethnic State of Manipur. This idea is promoted by the urban elite of Manipur.

The second factor is the Indian apathy towards the political aspirations of the people of Manipur. There were three segments of society in Manipur holding different political opinions at the time of merger of the State into India in 1949. The peasant revolutionaries under the leadership of Hijam Irabot Singh had started a fight for the establishment of a sovereign Socialist Republic in Manipur and some parts of Upper Burma. The second opinion was that of the urban elitist Congress leaders who wanted integration with India as they were influenced and attracted to the Indian nationalism projected through the personalities of national leaders like Mahatma Gandhi and Jawaharlal Nehru. The third group, meek and silent were the Meitei nationalists who wanted to maintain a vague idea of independent and separate political entity of Manipur with the continuation of the existing constitutional status and treaty relation with India. The movement for integration of India sponsored by pro-India nationalists succeeded while the Communist revolt of Irabot Singh failed. The Meitei nationalists did not react, remained silent and sulky.[16] After the controversial merger which led to the abolition of constitutional monarchy of Manipur, contrary to the expectation of the Congress leaders the Government of India followed a veiled policy of colonialism; a replacement of the British colonial rule by the Central Government rule of India. Manipur was denied of her democratic rights and institutions. Manipur was downgraded as a Part C State and Union Territory. The demand of the people for the restoration of the Legislative Assembly was ignored for a long time. Meanwhile the issue of the political integrity of Manipur was raised by regional and national political parties. The Socialist party wanted Manipur to be merged with the province of Assam as a district. This proposal was opposed by different political elements of Manipur. In 1954, the State Reorganisation Commission also recommended the merger of Manipur into the State of Assam. Downgrading the political status of Manipur from a monarchical State to a district of an Indian State was disliked and opposed by the people of Manipur. Meanwhile the nationalists formed a political party known as Manipur National Union to demand a full-fledged State for

Manipur. The founding of this revolutionary party was suppressed by the imprisonment of its leaders like Sagolsem Indramani Singh and Yangmaso Shaiza but it imbibed the idea of separatism among the youth of Manipur. The leaders of Manipur irrespective of party affiliation were disillusioned at the apathy of the political leaders and the Government of India towards the political future of Manipur. Instead of a responsible government, Manipur was given a bureaucratic government under the central rule. This dissatisfaction of the political leaders was responsible for opening a door to the revolutionary movements among the youth of Manipur.

The central administration was unfortunately inefficient, corrupt and unpopular. Many of the revolutionary leaders accused that they were victims of bureaucratic corruption during the Union Territory administration. The government machinery was manned by officers sent by New Delhi. They happened to be all outsiders who did not speak the local language. A political party described the domination of the administration by outsider as 'Demanipurization' of the Government. A revolution always happened as a movement against the outsiders. Xenophobia or anti outside feeling in most cases was a cause of revolution. It happened in Manipur also. Most of the ills of Manipur have been attributed to the inordinately long central rule. However these did not absolve the political leaders of the national parties for the failure to provide democratic freedom to the State.

To the political frustration of the people are added the miseries of economic stagnancy and exploitation by an unholy alliance between big business, corrupt bureaucracy and pliant political leadership. The economic exploitation and policy of internal colonialism are the greatest factors for the cause of economic misery to the common people. During the pre-colonial period the foreign traders were the dominant mercantile community who exploited the people in collusion with colonial authorities. In the post colonial period there was an inflow of outside traders in Manipur. They were favoured by the Indian officers of the Manipur administration and they controlled the trade and commerce of the State and monopolized the Government expenditure. This was simply economic exploitation of the people which created a great discontentment. The government both at the centre and the Union Territory followed a policy which is condemned as internal colonialism. The central government invested money in Manipur as financial grants which were used for purchasing goods and commodities from mainland capitalists. This internal colonial economy greatly affected the economic condition of the people. The huge fund allocation of the government has gone to the contractors and big business. The emergence of an affluent class of contractors, engineers and big business was a disturbing social phenomenon in Manipur. Their involvement in politics especially during ministry making has commercialized the politics of Manipur. Further there was no industrial development worth to name. It was a consumer oriented economy. People were helpless at this working of internal colonialism. Meanwhile educated unemployment was increasing. The unemployment of the youth with bureaucratic non concern could be taken as an important direct cause of the youth revolution. Further it should be noted that the bureaucracy does not have a will to meet the challenges of the revolution.

The political parties and leaders who believed in the ideals of Indian constitution organized a non violent agitation for the grant of statehood for Manipur. This demand was not acceded to the people on the ground of non viability of Manipur as a State and lack of experience in the working of democratic institutions. Manipur was given a Union Territorial Council and Territorial Assembly whereas the Naga Hills district where a violent disturbance were created by the Naga insurgents was granted a full fledged State within the Indian republic in 1963. The leaders and people of Manipur greatly resented this policy of Central Government though the two units presented themselves as two different categories of political movements. One was an armed rebellion and the other was a peaceful and democratic agitation. A large number of youth who were politically aware went towards revolutionary movement during this period of political wilderness of Manipur.

Lastly there grew up a number of youth who were educated in India's metropolitan cities who came into contact with several revolutionary elements were drawn towards this highly discontented political and social situation of Manipur. This section of the youth led the different outfits which organized the revolutionary movements in Manipur.[17] The following are the important national movements which are regarded as revolutionary in nature:

(i) Communist Revolutionary Movement

(ii) The Meitei State Committee

(iii) United National Liberation Front (UNLF)

(iv) Revolutionary Government of Manipur (RGM)

(v) Peoples' Liberation Army (PLA)

(vi) Peoples' Revolutionary Party of Kangleipak (PREPAK)

(vii) Kangleipak Communist Party (KCP)

(viii) Kanglei Yawol Kanna Lup (KYKL)

The Communist Revolutionary Movement (1948-51)

The first armed revolutionary movement was started by the legendary leader Hijam Irabot Singh in 1948 and it continued till 1951. In 1948, the attention of the political parties in northeast was actively drawn to the proposal of creation of a new State named Purvanchal (Northeastern Province) consisting of Manipur, Tripura, Cachar and Lushai Hills. The proposal was sponsored by the Congress leaders of Bengal. Irabot and political parties of Manipur were opposed to this proposal. He organized a protest meeting of the Krishak Sabha at MDU Hall of Imphal on 21st September, 1948. Accidentally a group of Krishak Sabha workers who came from northern Iril River valley had scuffled with a contingent of Manipur police leading to the death of Naran Singh.

This unprecedented incident led to the banning of the protest meeting and order of arrest of Irabot Singh who went underground from that day onwards. One month before this fateful incident, Irabot organized a district committee of the Communist Party of India for Manipur. He was admonished for not establishing a branch of the Communist Party of India under the provincial committee of Assam. He made a confession on his activities regarding the organization of the Communist Party in Manipur known as Circular Number 8.

Irabot Singh was directed to organize a revolution of the working class as per thesis of B.T. Ranadive adopted in the second Congress of CPI in 1948 in Calcutta. He was not fully convinced of the workability of this revolution of the workers because Manipur was an agrarian country of peasants and not of workers. Irabot Singh meanwhile was elected to the Manipur Legislative Assembly from Utlou constituency but he did not attend any session of the Assembly. He was wanted by the State for being indulging in violent activities. After sometime the Communist Party renounced Ranadive's thesis of working class revolution and his thesis were replaced by the party's Chinese thesis of peasant revolution. At that time Irabot Singh, as a head of the Communist party in Manipur started organizing the peasant revolution. The members of the Krishak Sabha became the members of the Communist Party and fully backed him in the revolution. He organized the Red Guards, the fighting arms of the revolution. A number of university educated youth were trained for armed insurrection. The Government of India and the State authorities of Manipur after the merger of Manipur to the Dominion of India carried out counter measures to suppress the revolution. The Indian Army, the Assam Rifles and the Manipur Police carried out repressive activities. There were casualties on both sides. Irabot Singh went to Upper Chindwin district in Kabaw Valley of Burma and tried to extend the revolutionary activities in this area. He tried to reconcile the factions of the Burmese Communist Party into a united front. His political programme in this revolution was the creation of a Socialist republic in Manipur and the areas of his control in Burma. Unfortunately due to the non-availability of medical treatment, Irabot Singh died of typhoid in the village of Tangbo in Upper Burma on 26th September 1951. Meanwhile the police organized large scale suppressive measures to suppress the activities of the communist revolutionaries. The communist revolutionaries were captured and tried in a case known as the Manipur Conspiracy Case, 1952. The involved leaders were given heavy punishment of imprisonment. The death of Irabot Singh coincided with the suppression of the Communist revolt. The Communist Party of India also changed its ideology of accepting the Indian constitution and becoming a lawful political party of India. The Communists of Manipur became the members of the Manipur State Council of Communist Party of India. The first revolutionary movement under the Communist Party of Manipur failed. However the legacy of H. Irabot Singh was picked up by some young leaders after his death. His followers became over ground members of the Communist Party and they participated in the electoral politics of Manipur before and after statehood.[18]

The Meitei State Committee (1967-1971)

The Meitei State Committee was a small organization consisting of a few former followers of Hijam Irabot Singh, the leader of the Communist revolution. The Meitei State Committee was formed by seven members on 12th January 1967 at the Naga village of Thangal Surung in Sadar Hills. The idea of an armed organization came up in early 1966 when a group of Meitei youth from Chandrakhong and Ukhongsang villages who were deputed by some Naga underground leaders of Manipur to contact the former revolutionaries of the armed revolt of 1948. Their sole objective was to make an understanding for the preservation of identity of the people of Manipur. They met Wangkheirakpam Tomba Singh who was a former associate of Hijam Irabot Singh and conveyed to him the desire of the Naga underground leaders to have an understanding with the Meitei of Manipur valley. Tomba Singh welcomed the proposal because he remembered the political line of his leader Irabot Singh who always strived for the creation of a social and political set up with the hill people through an armed struggle. Irabot Singh hoped for a close cooperation between the Meiteis and the hill people. Tomba Singh wanted to carry out the wish of his leader to have cooperation with the hill people and he agreed to the setting up of a revolutionary party to implement the ideology of Hijam Irabot Singh. He welcomed the proposal of the Naga underground to have a common front between the Nagas and the Meiteis. It has been reported that the initiative of the Naga Federal Government to have connection with the Meiteis was taken up by two Thangal Naga leaders, S. Punshi, a former Tatar (M.P) of Naga Hoho and Abung Thangal, the Khullakpa of Thangal Surung village who were friendly towards them. Tomba Singh went to Thangal village and he proceeded to Nagaland to have a talk with the Naga leaders. The Naga leaders expressed their desire to have solidarity between the Nagas and the Meiteis. They informed him to contact Sagolsem Indramani Singh of Thangmeiband Imphal who had established contact with the Naga leaders. Tomba Singh returned from Nagaland and requested some scholars to write a brief account of Meitei Naga relationship. The book was translated into English and sent to the Naga leaders. Ultimately both sides agreed to organize an armed movement against the government of Manipur. Tomba Singh formed a preparatory committee of 25 members to organize a political movement in the political line of Hijam Irabot Singh. In October 1966 a meeting of the preparatory committee was held in Wakhong village and the meeting decided to establish an armed revolutionary organization under the name of Manipur State Committee. The name was changed to Meitei State Committee on the suggestion of the Naga leaders that the revolutionary organization should work for the liberation of the Meiteis in the valley of Manipur. Another meeting was held at Thangal Surung village which ultimately decided to form the organization named Meitei State Committee in a four days meeting from 11-13 January, 1967.

The objective of the Meitei State Committee was to establish an independent State in Manipur.[19] The committee would join hands with other revolutionary groups in the States of northeast region.

Tomba Singh further negotiated with the Naga leaders who gave some small arms to the Meitei State Committee. The Meitei State Committee had two important wings; civil and military. The military wing was put under the command of a three men committee. The majority of the members of the armed wing were recruited from the ex-members of the revolutionary movement of 1948. They organized training of armed personnel at an underground Naga camp at Maram village. One Ito Singh was appointed Commander-in-Chief. The volunteers established a base camp at Purum Likli. Unfortunately the information of their whereabouts was leaked out to the government. A large police force was sent to encounter the revolutionaries. The police party attacked on the volunteers of the committee at a place called Purum Ching. In this attack Commander-in-Chief, Ito Singh was killed and a large number of volunteers were arrested. Sixty-three members were arrested and the police recovered many arms and explosives. The death of Ito Singh was a great set back to the Meitei State Committee and their activities declined. The State government of Manipur took advantage of this decline and tried to create dissensions among the members. The government promised financial payment to those leaders who surrendered to the police. The police also arrested W. Tomba Singh, the leader of the Meitei State Committee and his colleague Mohori Singh. He was put into jail till 1971. The government put down the Meitei State Committee by the end of 1972.

The Meitei State Committee failed because the leaders of the Committee were not intellectually well-equipped to organize a revolution. They lacked resources to organize their armed wing to fight against the State. Their relationship with the underground Nagas was not put on a sound level and the educated class of the Meiteis did not accept the Meitei-Naga revolutionary action. The propaganda of the State Government was effective to convince any observers to think that the members of the committee were "disoriented" left wing elements.[20] Only positive outcome of the insurrection of the Meitei State Committee is a legacy of faint idea of Manipuri nationalism was left behind.[21]

United National Liberation Front (1964)

The major revolutionary organization for the liberation of the people of Manipur from the colonial rule of India was established on 24th November, 1964 when the United National Liberation Front (UNLF) was established with a coordinating committee which consisted of the following Naga, Kuki and Meitei leaders:

1. Kalanlung Kamei, President
2. Thankhopao Singsit, Vice-President
3. Arambam Samarendra, General Secretary
4. Dr. Longjam Manimohan, Member
5. Laishram Kanhai, Member.
6. Nongmeikapam Sanajaoba, Member
7. Nongmaithem Pahari, Member

The President was Kalanlung Kamei, a Naga leader from Khoupum valley of Tamenglong district. The Vice-president was Thankhopao Singsit of Ehangkarong of Saikul sub division. The General Secretary, Arambam Samarendra who was a youth leader, playwright and sportsman was the leader of the UNLF. It was due to his leadership that both the Naga and Kuki leaders were in the leadership of the UNLF. Kalanlung Kamei in his lifetime did not disclose his deep connection with the front. He became involved in the movement for statehood and integrity of Manipur. He became an MLA when Manipur became a State in 1972. He died in 1995. Thankhopao Singsit was a committed Kuki leader who stood for unity and integrity of the people of Manipur. He was shot dead by an unknown person. Dr. Longjam Manimohan Singh was a follower of the revolutionary leader, Hijam Irabot Singh. He was involved in the Communist revolution of 1948-51. Nonmeikapam Sanajaoba (popularly known as N.K. Sanajaoba) was a popular youth leader and a journalist who always stood for integrity of Manipur and a corruption less society in the State. Nongmaithem Pahari was a well known singer and artist whose lyrics on patriotism inspired the people of Manipur towards nationalism. After the retirement of Kalanlung Kamei and Thankhopao Singsit from the revolutionary activities, Arambam Samarendra became the president of the UNLF. This front enjoyed sympathy and support from urban elite of Manipur. The UNLF as the name implies aim at the national liberation of Manipur. They also stand for Manipuri nationalism. The UNLF is one of the oldest revolutionary organizations in India. Their concept of Manipuri nationalism requires some amplification. The term Manipuri nationalism covers the nationalism of three ethnic communities of Manipur, the Meitei, the Naga and the Kuki. Nationalism in the opinion of Walker Connor means loyalty to one's ethnic group and loyalty and devotion to the multi ethnic State. Manipuri nationalism would mean loyalty to each one of the three ethnic groups and loyalty to the multi-ethnic State of Manipur. This is the ideological stand of the UNLF. The front condemns the Indian Government rule in Manipur as Indian colonial rule which had led to the decadence of Manipuri society. They wanted the restoration of the national independence of Manipur. Their objective was to carry out a national peoples' democratic revolution.

After the establishment of the organization, the leaders were engaged in the expansion and consolidation among different peoples and groups of Manipur. In the beginning they tried to contact the leaders of the Meitei State Committee to have a joint front with the UNLF. The Meitei State Committee refused to join the UNLF. Through the efforts of the Vice-President, Thankhopao Singsit who was a Kuki chief of Ehangkarong tried to mobilize the Kuki and Mizo people. Thankhopao was a believer in Manipuri nationalism. As an important representative of the UNLF, he met the Mizo leader, Laldenga for cooperation between Mizo National Front (MNF) and the UNLF. Laldenga is reported to have assured Thankhopao to send the General Secretary of the MNF to Manipur to continue the discussion. Another Kuki leader who supported the

UNLF was Lalkhohen who desired a greater Manipur and wanted quick action. His enthusiastic proposal was deferred by the UNLF and he joined the MNF to support Laldenga.

The leadership of the UNLF, after the ideological preparation decided to take help from the foreign powers. They approached the Chinese Government the reason being that China had ideological difference with India and they thought they could launch a revolution with the help and cooperation with the Chinese Government. They tried to contact the Chinese Embassy in Delhi through a Cambodian student named, Rev. Pen Sawen who was a volunteer of the Vietminh guerilla. The Chinese Embassy did not respond despite their attempts. Then they looked towards Pakistan who had an unfriendly relation with India. They entrusted a leader named Oinam Sudhirkumar for this diplomatic engagement. Sudhirkumar had a Meitei relative named Oinam Mikoi Singh in East Pakistan. He used to visit East Pakistan very frequently. The UNLF contacted Oinam Mikoi Singh to make contact with the Government of Pakistan. Oinam Sudhirkumar and some important leaders went to East Pakistan. However they were arrested at a railway station. Sudhirkumar disclosed the purpose of his visit. The local authorities in East Pakistan informed Pakistan's Foreign Office of the visit. The Foreign Office of Pakistan agreed to treat them as the guests of government of Pakistan. And the UNLF leaders were brought to Dacca. They met some high officials of Pakistan Government and urged them to extend assistance for the revolution in Manipur. The Pakistan Government expressed their inability to help the Manipur revolutionaries. Pakistan was busy in monitoring the war between Egypt and Israel. They were escorted to the Pakistan border by security forces. But instead of leaving Pakistan, they tried to return to Dacca to meet the officials of the Chinese Consulate. They were arrested by the Pakistan police at Bhanughat Railway Station. They were escorted to Sylhet and they informed the officials their intention to visit the Chinese Consulate in Dacca. O. Sudhirkumar and his friends were taken to Dacca where they met the Chinese officials who did not express their opinion. Thus ended the mission of UNLF without any positive result.

In 1968 a rift developed among the rank and file of UNLF. The split of the organization was due to the attempt of O. Sudhirkumar to control the party. He was the foreign secretary of UNLF. By virtue of being a foreign secretary he went to Pakistan where his mission failed. His activities in Pakistan were carried out without information to the higher authorities of the UNLF. There was also difference of class among the members of the organization between the proletariat and middle class. it was also felt that the Pakistan Government did not show any inclination to support the Manipuri revolutionaries in the absence of military preparedness of the UNLF for which Sudhirkumar blamed the leadership. This split marked the first phase of the UNLF.

Revolutionary Government of Manipur (RGM)

The UNLF was split when a chunk of revolutionary members came out from the UNLF and formed an organization known as the Revolutionary Government of Manipur under the leadership of O. Sudhirkumar who was a Secretary of Foreign Affairs. Before the establishment of this outfit, O. Sudhirkumar made an attempt to bring several organizations like the South Eastern Peoples' Organization of Thoubal, The Kaibiron and some other small organizations under a common organization named South Eastern Hill Region Mongolian Federal Republic. He tried to persuade many tribal leaders to join this outfit and a consolidation committee was formed to bring all like minded groups under a common committee. Other members of the Consolidation Committee were Nameirakpam Bisheshwor Singh, R.K. Sanajaoba and W. Sanatomba Singh. And the committee constituted seven departments headed by a Director each: Foreign Affairs, Intelligence, Finance, Home Affairs, Defence, Publicity and Food and Communication. Sudhirkumar sent his team of revolutionary leaders to East Pakistan to persuade their authorities to help them. He found that the attitude of the Pakistan Government, though not hostile, was non committal. So O. Sudhirkumar was compelled by circumstances of obtaining diplomatic lobby in Pakistan to establish "The Revolutionary Government of Manipur" (RGM) at Sylhet in the year 1969. Perhaps due to communication gap between O. Sudhirkumar and his colleagues of Manipur or miscalculations of the attitude of the Pakistan Government, a group of 200 Meitei volunteers went to East Pakistan without any valid documents. The Pakistan police arrested the volunteers on 1st July, 1969 at a place known as Bhanubil and were brought to Kamalganj Thana and kept at the Dak Bungalow near the police station. They were shifted to Maulavi Bazaar police station. They were all imprisoned in Sylhet Jail. On 30th July, 1969 the volunteers were escorted by East Pakistan Rifles to the border area to go back to India. These volunteers who were pushed into the Union Territory of Tripura in India were arrested by Tripura police in the first week of August 1969. Kailasar police station arrested 34 volunteers and Dharamnagar police arrested 22 volunteers. And the Government of Manipur started a criminal case of conspiracy against all these revolutionaries "who had gone to East Pakistan to receive training in arms for the purpose of overthrowing the Government of Manipur by an armed revolution making Manipur a sovereign State outside Indian Union.[22]

O. Sudhirkumar, the leader of the Revolutionary Government of Manipur, after the deportation of the volunteers to Tripura of India, stayed behind in East Pakistan. He and other eight colleagues secretly avoided crossing over to India. He went to Dacca where he met highly ranking military officers of Pakistan. He convinced the Pakistani military authorities of his mission. The Pakistani authorities gave arms training to the eight volunteers at the Borlekha Commando Training Centre in Sylhet district. The training continued till the Bangladesh war in 1970-71. The war gave a great setback to the Manipuri revolutionaries. After the defeat of Pakistan army, they returned to India. They had several encounters with Indian army and CRPF in the western boundaries of Manipur, Jiribam and Nungba area on the National Highway 53.

The volunteers were all rounded up by Manipur police. Thus by 1971 the attempt of the RGM for a military revolution to establish a sovereign government of Manipur failed. Meanwhile the Manipur police took up repressive measures against the RGM. They arrested N. Pahari Singh, the Chief of the Army Staff of the Manipur Revolutionary. N. Pahari Singh was a very popular young man with a great attractive personality. He was later on released after imprisonment. The police arrested 123 volunteers and put them into jail. This period coincided with the height of political movement for statehood of Manipur. It produced a demoralizing effect on the revolutionaries. For example, 23 volunteers from Imphal Jail requested the Lt. Governor of Manipur to set them free and they assured him to give up their activities. The RGM lost the momentum of their movement and were defeated by the police. Several leaders of the RGM were given amnesty by the Government of Manipur when a new ministry led by the Manipur Peoples' Party came into power in 1972. O. Sudhirkumar after being granted amnesty continued to be involved in several social and constructive activities. He was shot dead by some unknown faction of revolutionaries. His organizing capacity and attractive personality aroused the national feeling of the Meitei revolutionaries.

The UNLF Again

After the failure of the RGM, the UNLF continued its political activities. In the 70s and 80s of the 20th century the UNLF concentrated mainly on mobilization and recruitment. Soon after its formation, the UNLF leaders established political relations with the Government of East Pakistan which provided military training to some of its cadre. This group supported the Pakistan army during 1971 Bangladesh war. They developed a relationship with China. In June 1975, N. Biseshwor Singh and others proceeded to Lhasa in Tibet to seek Chinese assistance. In 1990 it decided to launch an armed struggle for the liberation of Manipur from India. They also formed an armed wing known as Manipur Peoples' Army (MPA). On 22 May 1990, the UNLF along with other insurgent groups operating in the North East – the National Socialist Council of Nagaland – Khaplang (NSCN-K), the United Liberation Front of Asom (ULFA) and Kuki National Army (KNA) floated a pan-Mongoloid coalition called the Indo-Burma Revolutionary Front (IBRF) to wage a united struggle for the independence of these groups. The UNLF established training camps in Myanmar and Bangladesh. The political objective of the UNLF was the establishment of an independent socialist Manipur.

On 23 November A.D. 2000 the UNLF on its 36th Foundation Day reiterated the demand for liberation of the oppressed people from the Indian Union. An incident of great importance happened on 10th June, A.D. 2000 when it's Chairman, Arambam Samarendra Singh the founder and Chairman of the UNLF was shot dead by dissident group at Imphal. Arambam Samarendra was an ideologue of Manipuri nationalism and Manipur revolution. The UNLF through its military wing, the Manipur Peoples' Army had been operating throughout Manipur. After the death of the founder leadership of the UNLF was taken up by Rajkumar Meghen Singh alias Sana Yaima as the Chairman of UNLF. The UNLF continues to operate outside India and maintains close links with militant outfits in India. This is the strongest ongoing revolutionary group of Manipur.

Peoples' Liberation Army (1978-1981)

The Peoples' Liberation Army (PLA) was established on 25th September, 1978 at a place called Nongpok Sekmai under the leadership of N. Biseshwor Singh who was one of the founding leaders of the United National Liberation Front (UNLF). The PLA plans to organize a revolutionary front covering the entire north east India and unite all the ethnic groups therein including, the Meiteis, Nagas and Kukis. N. Joykumar observes on this organization, "The biggest asset of this organization was its ideology. It strongly emphasized for the establishment of a classless society based on the principle of Marxism. This ideological aspect was a distinctive departure from the ideological concept of the previous revolutionary organizations. At the same time, the main objective of the organization was to establish a distinctive separate political identity of the entire States of North Eastern Region outside the Indian Union."[23] Biseshwor Singh was closely associated with O. Sidhirkumar since RGM's activities in Pakistan. The two developed differences after the failure of the RGM. Sudhirkumar was pro-America and wanted to observe the international situation before plunging into further activities. N. Biseshwor was a Marxist ideologically and was pro-Chinese with whose help he wanted to organize a revolution. He left Manipur for Lhasa in Tibet with 15 youths via Gorakhpur (Bihar) and Nepal in April, 1976. According to another account the number of youth who went to Lhasa was 20.[24] The experience of Manipuri PLA trainees was not happy at the dictatorial attitude of the Chinese instructor. N. Biseshwor and his group returned to Manipur after a period of three months. However he adopted the Marxist ideology in this attempted liberation of Manipur. The PLA was commanded by a small apex body named the Executive Body consisting of 7 members who were N. Biseshwor Singh, Chairman, Biramangol, Temba, Chirom Ranjit, Rajen Achouba, Rajen Macha and Kabichandra.

The PLA established linkages with several militant organizations in the north east. The PLA recruits were trained in guerilla warfare by the undivided National Socialist Council of Nagaland at its headquarter in Challam beyond the Somra tract in north Myanmar in 1980's. PLA also established contact with Pakistan's Inter Services Intelligence (ISI). The PLA applied the theory of elimination of its rivals. PLA killed O. Sudhirkumar who was a leader of RGM on 14th January 1978. The PLA thought that the group of Sudhirkumar was a gang of counter revolutionaries who became hostile to the revolutionaries. PLA claimed the assassination of Sudhirkumar as a great achievement. In 1979 the PLA formed a political body called the Revolutionary Peoples' Front (RPF). The PLA had several attacks on the security forces like the SSB, Home Guards, Border Security Forces, and Village Volunteer Force. They also established training centres at

Baruni Chingkhong, Natum Ching and Keibi. The PLA got a great setback on 6th July, 1981 when their camp at Tekcham was attacked by the Army which resulted into the killing of several hard core leaders and capture of N. Biseshwor Singh, the legendary leader of the PLA. The PLA leaders who lost their lives were Biramangol Singh, Indrajit, Khogen, Rajen Macha, Inao, Shanti. After undergoing imprisonment for several years, N. Biseshwor Singh contested election to the Manipur Legislative Assembly. As a member of the Assembly, Biseshwor Singh desired to evolve a legislative revolution. A few years afterward he was killed by some of his former colleagues.

After the capture of Biseshwor Singh by the army and his electoral political career, the PLA was led by Irengbam Chaoren Singh who was made the President of the RPF which runs a government in exile in Bangladesh. Some of his cadres operate in Myanmar also. PLA established in the end of the 20th century, two camps in Myanmar and five camps in Bangladesh. It is an ongoing revolutionary organization.

Peoples' Revolutionary Party of Kangleipak (1977-85)

The Peoples' Revolutionary Party of Kangleipak popularly known as PREPAK is an armed revolutionary group in Manipur demanding a separate and independent homeland to be called Kangleipak. The PREPAK was formed under the leadership of Rajkumar Tulachandra, a youth leader of Thangmeiband of Imphal on 9th October 1977. This was a clear case of publicized ethnicity assertiveness of the Meitei nation. Meitei nationalism was the basis of the revolutionary programme of PREPAK. The PREPAK was formed in a meeting held at a hillock called Cheiraoching of Langol Hills in northern Imphal. The meeting was attended by youth leaders namely, R.K. Tulachandra, S. Wanglen, Achamba, Tajila, Meiraba, Maipaksana, Y. Ibohanbi. After its formation the PREPAK carried out attacks and ambushes on the security forces of Manipur known as the Manipur Police and Manipur Rifles. There was a split in the organization. A group led by Y. Ibohanbi defected from PREPAK and formed the Kangleipak Communist Party (KCP). The PREPAK started with enthusiasm. They had a 13-point programme to fight against colonial forces and internal colonialism of India. Their objective was to establish a socialist society in Manipur after a successful armed revolution. The Government of Manipur could effectively deal with the PREPAK. R.K. Tulachandra Singh on whose head Government announced a sum of Rs. 25,000 was arrested by the police on June 1979. He escaped from the police custody of Singjamei Police Station. The escape of Tulachandra was a sensation in Manipur. He was rearrested in 19th February 1980 and he was persuaded by the Governemnt to make an appeal to the PREPAK to surrender through his message from the All India Radio. He appealed to his colleagues to support the Government of Chief Minister Rajkumar Dorendra Singh. The PREPAK refused to respond positively to the appeal of Tulachandra Singh. A faction of PREPAK led by Maipak Sharma also supported the Government. The PREPAK could make contact with Mizo National Front of Mizoram and Tripura National Volunteer (TNV) of Tripura. The PREPAK as a revolutionary organization had declined by 1985. However Tulachandra Singh after his release from jail tried to reorganize the PREPAK and take up an armed action.

The founding leader of PREPAK, R.K. Tulachandra was killed in an encounter with the police at the village of Kabowakching on 12th November, 1985. After his death, S. Wanglen became the Commander-in-Chief of the PREPAK. The group suffered from factionalism; therefore some of the members joined other revolutionary groups like the PLA and UNLF. A leader of PREPAK Meiraba alias Urikhengbam Sarat tried to unite the PREPAK with the help of UNLF and PLA. After the reunification of its members the PREPAK launched a social reformation campaign in the State of Manipur like the eradication of social crimes against women, drug and alcohol addiction. In 1993 PREPAK suffered a setback when its General Secretary, L. Masunga was killed. After the death of Masunga a founding member of PREPAK named Paliba was elected General Secretary. Tajila was appointed Commander-in-Chief and Chinglenba Mangang was appointed the Defence Secretary. Soon they were split into two factions, one faction led by Paliba the General Secretary and the other led by Vice-Chairman Naba. There were factional clashes between the groups resulting into death of several members. Other revolutionary groups like UNLF, PLA, KYKL and KCP tried to unite them again.[25]

Kangleipak Communist Party (1979-95)

The Kangleipak Communist Party (KCP) was founded on 20th August, 1979 at a Tangkhul Naga village of Mapao. It was established under the leadership of Yendrenbam Ibohanbi popularly known as Baji. The exact date of the foundation of this party is disputed. Yendrenbam Ibohanbi was a founding leader of PREPAK but he defected from it to establish the KCP. The principle objective of the party was to establish an independent State of Kangleipak by removing Indian political parties, their agents and imperial forces. The KCP according to the leaders stands for the people of Manipur (Kangleipak), the entire people of the north eastern region of India, for the people of south east Asia and for the workers and peasants of independent States based on classless society. They claim to be the successors of the legacy of Communist Irabot Singh who organized Manipur revolution in the years 1948-51. The KCP however was not free from internal factions. Y. Ibohanbi Singh, the Commander-in-Chief of the Red Army of the KCP was the leader of the armed revolution. On 1st July 1995 there was an exchange of fire between the KCP and CRPF at a place called Heitupokpi near the village of Andro in the Nongmaiching Hills in which Y. Ibohanbi Singh was shot dead by CRPF. The KCP condemned this day as the black day. With the death of Y. Ibohanbi Singh the activities of KCP had gone into the hands of various younger leaders who broke up the KCP into different factions. The KCP is still an ongoing organization with lesser strength.

Kanglei Yawol Kanna Lup (1994)

Kanglei Yawol Kanna Lup (KYKL) meaning "the organization to save the revolutionary movement in Manipur" is a Meitei revolutionary group formed in January 1994 after the merger of the Oken faction of the UNLF, the Meiraba faction of PREPAK and Ibopishak faction of KCP. The objective of the KYKL is to build the Meitei society by clearing it of all vices like immoral activities, drug trade and corruption. This group stands for 'nationalism' of the entire north eastern region to be based on the principle of "all for one and one for all". The outfit launched "Operation New Kangleipak" (ONK), an anti-corruption campaign to clean up the education system in Manipur. It has also pledged open support other militant outfits who work against the narcotic trades, drug addiction, immoral activities and corruption in society.

The outfit received certain setback when two of its top leaders, Chairman N. Oken and Commander-in-Chief N. Thouba Singh were reportedly arrested without confirmation. In 1996 a number of cadres surrendered before the security forces and the KYKL was split into two – the KYKL (O) led by Namoijam Oken and KYKL (T) led by Achou Toijamba. However after five years of inter group rivalry the Oken and Toijamba factions decided to reunite in February 2002. The united KYKL formed an adhoc central executive committee with Achou Toijamba as Chairman and Keisham Yaima as the General Secretary. It also formed a military commission known as Meeyamgi Yawol Lanmee (MYL) which is jointly headed by Namoijam Oken and Toijam Ibochou. Keirungba Khuman was the deputy finance secretary in whose name the demand notes to the general public were issued and funds were collected. The KYKL has close linkages with the NSCN (IM). They also had nexus with Zomi Revolutionary Army (ZRA) ans Meghalaya based Achik National Volunteer Council (ANVC). KYKL also maintains links with the Khaplang faction of the NSCN for training and shelter to KYKL cadres from its bases in Myanmar. The KYKL operates widely in the Manipur valley and Myanmar and in several cities in India.

Government's Response

The response of the Government of India and State Government of Manipur in the initial stage was the military suppression of the revolutionary outfits. They had successfully suppressed the early armed revolutionary movement of Hijam Irabot Singh. The Meitei State Committee which was a legacy of H. Irabot's Communist movement which was inspired by the Naga revolutionaries were also suppressed by the State police. The Revolutionary Government of Manipur, a phase and the outfit of the United National Liberation Front also failed. The granting of Statehood to Manipur in 1972 gave an opportunity to the regional party (Manipur Peoples' Party) leadership to grant amnesty to the leaders of the UNLF and the functionaries of the Revolutionary Government of Manipur. The amnesty granted by the State government provided a respite for the revolutionary groups either to reorganize or form separate outfits to continue their activities. While the revolutionary groups took advantage of the freedom given by the amnesty, they were either too weak or disunited to negotiate with the authorities. The leaders of the Government of India and the State government (including central ministers, governors and chief ministers) offered negotiation with the various groups of revolutionaries. One chief minister succeeded to persuade some revolutionary leaders to support the State government. The Indian Army backed by the paramilitary forces like the Assam Rifles, Border Security Force, CRPF and Manipur Rifles took up the repressive measures. They took advantage of the Armed Forces Special Power's Act (1958) which was originally used against the Naga rebels to suppress the Meitei revolutionary groups. The counter insurgency operations carried out by the security forces led to violation of human rights of the common people. There grew up civil society movements against the violation of human rights by security forces. The most prominent among these groups were the Meira Paibis (the women torch bearers) protesting against the military accesses, civil society organizations of human right activists. The greatest example of the human right protest movement is exemplified by the hunger strike of a woman protestor, Irom Sharmila. The government of

Manipur appealed to the revolutionary groups to come to a negotiation table. But most of them particularly the UNLF, PLA and KYKL took a firm stand against negotiation with the Government of India. They thought that this negotiation through cease fire or cessation of military operation would dilute their aim of sovereign Manipur. The Indian Army which was encouraged by the ceasefire between India and the Naga group led by two factions of the NSCN held out a peaceful stance towards the Meitei revolutionaries by winning over the people including intellectuals. Militarization of Manipur was going on. At the same time the Government of India followed a democratic policy of giving development to the people of Manipur. The stalemate continued by the end of the 20th century.

III

The Naga Ethno Nationalism

The Naga ethno nationalism is an outcome of the British colonialism, the Second World War and the Naga national movement. The British rule established the identity and the ethnic space of the Nagas. The Naga nationalists point to the establishment of the Naga Club in 1918 and their submission of a memorandum to the Simon Commission which clearly demanded that the future of the Nagas should not be linked up with the British government constitutional reforms for India. This was the beginning of the Naga political consciousness. The Second World War brought about tremendous changes in Naga politics, society and economy. It was followed by the establishment of a British sponsored Naga Hills District Tribal Council in 1945 under the direction of the Deputy Commission, Sir Charles Pawsey with the aim of uniting the Nagas and repairing some of the damages of the war. In March of the following year this council met at Wokha and renamed it as the Naga National Council in 1946. Regarding the effect of the Second World War on the Nagas T. Sakhrie the articulate leader of the Naga National Council wrote, "Up to the time of Japanese invasion in 1944 the Nagas had lived in an age of almost uninterrupted continuity with the past. The Nagas made a leap, as it were, from a distant past into the glare of the present century with the advent of the Japanese and found their world greatly changed. They looked about with uncertainty and pinched themselves to be reassured that all this was really true. . . . Suddenly they found themselves clamouring for more and more schools in which they saw social progress and, where Government could not build them, they went ahead to build their own. Existing schools were filled to overflowing:

> "People became suddenly restive with the existing State of affairs. There was social unrest, economic unrest, political unrest. Everywhere there were cries of better, bigger and nobler things. Things that were considered a luxury became the standard of the day. Trade received a new impetus, as indeed the era brought in a new impetus to all fields of human endeavour. . .
>
> "Standards of value and taste often changed. 'Foreign dress which, before the war, had been considered a luxury but in good taste, had to yield place to the artistic native dress on which the new nationalism had stamped its approval. Foreign culture had to make way for the native culture. National dances and native songs were restored to their original places of honour. . . . The clash of imperialistic interests had given birth to the new era – full of opportunities and hopes for a glorious future."[26]

NNC Memorandum to Viceroy Lord Mountbatten (1947)

The NNC submitted a memorandum on 20th February, 1947 to the Viceroy Lord Louis Mountbatten expressing the Naga aspiration for independence. It says, the memorandum seeks to present the case of the Naga people for self-determination for the realization of which an appeal is made to H.M.G. and the Government of India to set up for the Naga people an Interim Government for a period of 10 years at the end of which the Naga people will be left to choose any form of government under which they will live.

The memorandum pointed out three "thought provoking" factors as reproduced below:

(1) Ethnically the Nagas are from a distinct stock

(2) The Nagas have distinct social life, manner of living, laws and customs and even their method of governance of the people is quite different.

(3) In religion, the majority of the Nagas are Animists but Christianity which was introduced by the American Baptist long before the advent of the British is now speedily spreading. Such factors as the above make it imperative that Nagas have a separate form of Government.

Naga system of Administration

"The basis of the Naga system is the village organization. Every village is an independent unit in the tribe. Villages are managed by a Council of Elders and men of influence elected by the people. Such a polity, such a State of society and democratic life cannot be found in any part of India.

The Naga Case

The NNC was opposed to the Constituent Assembly of India drafting a constitution for whole country. The memorandum said,

> "A Constitution drawn up by the people who have no knowledge of the Naga Hills and the Nagas will be quite unsuitable and unacceptable to the Naga people...
>
> "This Memorandum is placed with the authorities for setting up of an Interim Government of the Naga people with financial provisions for a period of 10 years at the end of which the Naga people will be left to choose any form of government under which they themselves choose to live.[27]"

The arguments used by T. Sakhrie in this memorandum clearly established ethno national bonds of the Nagas as perceived by the NNC which described the Nagas as a nation seeking the right of self determination.

The Nine Point Agreement, 1947

Sir Akbar Hydari the Governor of Assam also went ahead to negotiate with the leaders of the NNC who were mostly government servants and an Agreement consisting of 9 points was concluded between him and the NNC. The Agreement is reproduced herewith.

Tribes represented at discussions on the 26th, 27th and 28th June, 1947, at Kohima were Western Angamis, Eastern Angamis, Kukis, Kacha Nagas (Mzemi), Rengmas, Semas, Lothas, Aos, Sangtams, Changs.

Heads of Proposed Understanding

That the right of the Nagas to develop themselves according to their freely expressed wishes is recognized.

1. *Judicial*: All cases whether civil or criminal arising between Nagas in the Naga Hills will be disposed of by duly constituted Naga Courts according to Naga customary law or such law as may be introduced with the consent of duly recognized Naga representative organizations: save that where a sentence of transportation or death has been passed there will be a right of appeal to the Governor.

   In cases arising between Nagas and non-Nagas in (a) Kohima and Mokokchung town areas, and (b) in the neighbouring plains districts the judge if not a Naga will be assisted by a Naga assessor.

2. *Executive*: The general principle is accepted that what the Naga Council is prepared to pay for the Naga Council should control. This principle will apply equally to the work done as well as the staff employed. While the District Officer will be appointed at the discretion of the Governor Subdivisions of the Naga Hills should be administered by a Sub-divisional Council with a full time executive President paid by Naga Council who would be responsible to the District Officer – for all matters falling within the

latter's responsibility, and to the Naga Council for all "-matters falling within their responsibility.

In regard to: (a) Agriculture – the Naga Council will exercise all the powers now vested in the District Officer, (b) P.W.D. – the Naga Council would take over full control, (c) Education and forest department – the Naga Council is prepared to pay for all the services and staff.

3. *Legislative*: That no laws passed by the provincial or central Legislature which would materially affect the terms of this agreement or the religious practices of the Nagas shall have legal force in the Naga Hills without the consent of the Naga Council. In cases of dispute as to whether any law did so affect this agreement the matter would be referred by the Naga Council to the Governor who would then direct that the law in question should not have legal force in the Naga Hills pending the decision of the Central Government.

4. *Land*: That land with all its resources in the Naga Hills should not be alienated to a non-Naga without the consent of the Naga Council.

5. *Taxation*: That the Naga Council will be responsible for the imposition, collection, and expenditure of land revenue and house tax and of such other taxes as may be imposed by the Naga Council.

6. *Boundaries*: That present administrative divisions should be modified so as (1) to bring back into the Naga Hills District all the forests transferred to the Sibsagar and Nowgong Districts in the past, and (2) to bring under one unified administrative unit as far as possible all Nagas. All the areas as included would be within the scope of the present proposed agreement. No areas should be transferred out of the Naga Hills without the consent of the Naga Council.

7. *Arms Act*: That Deputy Commissioner will act on the advice of the Naga Council in accordance with the provision of the Arms Act.
8. *Regulation*: "The Chin Hills Regulation and the Bengal Eastern Frontier Regulation" will remain in force.
9. *Period of Agreement*: The Governor of Assam as the Agent of the Government of the Indian Union will have a special responsibility for a period of 10 years to ensure the due observance of this agreement; at the end of this period the Naga Council will be asked whether they require the above agreement to be extended for a further period or a new agreement regarding the future of Naga people arrived at.

This agreement was associated with some controversies. Governor Akbar Hydari was happy over this achievement. He reported to Prime Minister Pandit Jawaharlal Nehru who was the Vice President of the Executive Council of the Viceroy of India on 7th July 1947. It was an understanding dealing with the future relationship of the Province (Naga Hills) with the Union Government. It gave considerable degree of local self government but retained all residuary powers with the Province of Assam and Union Government. This agreement also maintained the legal position of the Naga Hills as an integral part of Assam. The Governor recommended that in the best interest of the Province of Assam and the hill people this understanding should be accepted by the Government of India. Nehru congratulated the Governor for the success and observed, "The note on discussion and understanding arrived at Kohima will be sent to the Constituent Assembly". However on the advice of the Governor himself, to avoid public discussion on this issue the matter was not referred to the Constituent Assembly. This would have been sent to the Constituent Assembly.

A.Z. Phizo, the radical Naga nationalist was opposed to this Nine point understanding and he left for Delhi to meet Mahatma Gandhi and Sardar Vallabhai Patel. Phizo's interview with Mahtama

Gandhi was published in the *Dawn*, an organ of the Muslim League. There was controversy over the interpretation of Article 9 of the understanding. The NNC was divided into two groups, the moderates and the extremists. Phizo was the leader of the extremists who wanted independence of the Nagas to be declared on 14th August 1947. The NNC announced the declaration of Naga independence on 14th August 1947. A cable was sent to the Secretary General of the United Nations Organization.[28] The NNC now led by T. Aliba Imti as the President decided while endorsing the agreement to modify Article 9 of the Agreement as follows.

> "The Governor of Assam as the Agent of the Government of Indian Union will have a special responsibility for a period of 10 years to ensure the due observance of this agreement, at the end of this period the Nagas will be free to decide their own future."

The Deputy Commissioner, Sir Charles Pawsey suggested the following amendment.

> "At the end of this period the NNC would be free to decide what arrangements would be made for the future administration of the Naga country, it being understood that the Naga country must remain in the Indian Union."

The NNC submitted on 4th November 1947 an ultimatum to the Government of India that their proposal for the amendment of the Article 9 be accepted. It was also mentioned that if this ultimatum was not accepted,

> "the Naga people will not cooperate with the existing government, and Nagaland shall cease to be part of the Indian Union from 6th December 1947."

This ultimatum could not be endorsed due to lack of unanimity among the leaders of NNC. The Nagas were disappointed over the failure of the implementation of the 9 point agreement. The Governor Akbar Hydari and Premier Gopinath Bordaloi of Assam assured Phizo and his colleagues that the spirit of the agreement was incorporated in the draft constitution. Gopinath Bordaloi was a convenor of the sub committee of the Constituent Assembly on tribal autonomy. He visited Kohima and persuaded Phizo and other Naga leaders to accept the autonomy of the hill districts given in Schedule VI of the Draft Constitution. Schedule VI Autonomy was rejected by the Nagas. Meanwhile Phizo was elected the President of the NNC by defeating a moderate leader named Visar. Phizo was fully prepared for fighting for the independence of Nagaland.

Naga Voluntary Plebiscite (16th May, 1951)

A.Z. Phizo after becoming the fourth President of the NNC organized a plebiscite of all the Nagas whether they wanted independence or not of the Nagas. NNC informed the Government of India of its decision to hold the plebiscite and requested them to send observers whether plebiscite was held in proper or not. It was claimed by the NNC that the plebiscite was a great success and the Nagas put their thumb impression of approval on the declaration of the plebiscite. This plebiscite became a talking point for the Naga cause in India and abroad. Phizo's idea of Naga nationalism was explained in his address on the occasion of the Naga Voluntary Plebiscite held on Wednesday, 16th May 1951. He declared,

> "Being a nation, the Naga have their own distinct way of manners and living. In our country land belongs to the people as private property and every family possesses land. We uphold every person as sovereign: man and woman alike. Every family is a landlord; but there is no landlordism in Nagaland.
>
> "Democracy is the very spirit in our country. . . the system of our Naga community organization, which is rooted in the human principle of individual responsibility, sharing collectively the common weal and woe together, had stood the test of time throughout these centuries of great changes.
>
> "Nagas do not want to be associated with, much less to become citizens, of a people who have no sense of human honour in their make up, and no human compassion even towards their own sons and daughters. We must yet believe that the Indian leaders will adhere to Mahatma Gandhi's doctrine of 'Non-violence.'

He made a 10 point declaration "why do the Nagas want to be independent"?

He concluded the address with the following remarks "Above everything else, we want to be free as a distinct nation; and we shall be free.[29]"

Boycott of General Election

Encouraged by the "success" of the plebiscite, the NNC announced the boycott of the general election to the Assam provincial Assembly and Parliament of India. The boycott was supported by the people. Nobody filed the nomination for election to the Assembly and the Parliament though the Government of Assam made the preparation for the conduct of election. It was followed by two visits of Prime Minister Jawaharlal Nehru to Kohima in 1952 and 53. Due to the mishandling of the public relation by the Deputy Commissioner of Naga Hills, the request for submission of memorandum by the NNC to the Prime Minister was rejected by the Government of Assam. The Nagas who were ready to attend the public reception to be addressed by the Prime Minister boycotted the public meeting. This was greatly resented by Prime Minister Nehru in the front of Prime Minister U Nu of Burma. This fiasco strained the relation between the Government of India and NNC. The Government of Assam headed by Chief Minister Bisnu Ram Medhi failed to persuade the Naga leaders for amicable talks. In the general election of 1957, three Nagas filed nomination papers. There was no opposition and no voting and three of them were returned to Assam Legislative Assembly. One of them became the Deputy Minister.

The Naga Federal Government (1956)

The tempo of hostility increased between the Government of Assam and the NNC. The government employees, especially the Naga employees were threatened, denounced and attacked by the cadres of the NNC. In March 1956, the leaders of the NNC founded the Naga Federal Government and its flag was hoisted on 22nd March, 1956 at the Rengma village of Phensinyu. The NNC adopted a constitution (Yezhabo) of the Federal Government. It provided a government of the Naga areas. It also established an elaborate military organization of Naga Home Guards. The armed cadre of the Naga Army used the arms left behind by the Japanese during the Second World War. They started rebellion in the district and in Tuensang division of NEFA. It was spread to neighbouring Manipur and Assam. The Government utilized the services of Assam Police and Assam Rifles to suppress the rebellion. The rebels received in the beginning a good deal of support from the common people. Acts of violence were committed by both sides. The Government of India ordered army operations in Naga Hills. There were serious fighting between the army and the rebels during 1956 and 1957.

The Rise of Naga Liberalism

There were from the very beginning of the Naga movement two groups, the moderate and the extremist. One stood for a working administrative relation with India and the other separation from India. When the NNC started using violent means of fighting against the Indian military authorities, some elements were for adoption of non violent means of agitation. A serious division occurred between the majority led by A.Z. Phizo for a war of resistance or liberation from the Indian rule and a minority group who wanted peaceful non violent means for their political objectives. T. Sakhrie who was the most articulate spokesman of the Nagas started having difference with the radical group led by Phizo. In January 1956, T. Sakhrie was kidnapped and killed by the rebels. Some liberal leaders did not want the use of violence and condemned the militant movement. The Government of India was in favour of ending the conflict. In the later part of 1956, some of the liberal leaders met the Prime Minister who assured them to grant maximum autonomy on the condition of cessation of violent activities. Any political settlement should be preceded by restoration of peace. The liberal leaders mainly thought of bringing violence to an end. A Naga Peace Committee was formed in 1956 and it appealed to the people to abandon the policy of violence. In early 1956 some members of the Church came forward to appeal for peace. In the summer of this year, an All Tribes Naga

Peoples' Convention was held in Kohima between 22-26 August, 1957. The Convention was attended by 1765 delegates and 2,000 visitors. The convention which came to be known as the Naga Peoples' Convention (NPC) advocated a negotiated settlement of the Naga problem and suggested that pending a final political solution, the Naga Hills District of Assam and the Tuensang Frontier Division of NEFA should be constituted into a single administrative unit. The NPC leaders were hopeful that the rebels would come forward overground to join them. Dr. Verrier Elwin described the assertion of the moderate opinion as the rise of Naga liberalism. He said,

> "The essential importance of this meeting was that for the first time after the troubles began, a large number of Nagas declared their opposition to violence, and adopted constitutional means to achieve their political object.[30]"

In response to the positive approach of the NPC, the Government of India agreed to form a Union Territory to be named Naga Hills Tuensang Area (NHTA) under the Ministry of External Affairs to be administered by the Governor of Assam in his discretion as the agent of the President of India. The Union Territory was established on 1st December 1957. It was the first political response from the Government of India. The Government also declared a general amnesty for the release of convicts and prisoners. The new administration gave an impetus to those who lost faith in violence. It is reported that 3,000 rebels surrendered and 3,000 came over ground voluntarily; 4,000 prisoners were released under the terms of amnesty.[31]

A second Naga Peoples' Convention was held at Ungma, a very large village near Mokokchung in May 1958. Despite the threat from the Naga rebels, the convention was held. The NPC leaders were hopeful that the FGN leaders would cooperate with them on a united all Naga basis in drafting a proposal for a final settlement and a liaison committee was appointed to contact them. The attempt to win over the FGN leaders failed and the second convention appointed a drafting committee to formulate their constitutional demands. They also insisted that the Government of India should leave the door open for the NNC leaders to join them in drafting the document. The drafting committee prepared a 16-point memorandum for the constitution of a separate State to be named Nagaland within the Indian Union.

The third meeting of the Naga Peoples' Convention was held at Mokokchung in October 1959. The demand formulated by the delegates at the convention was formation of a separate State to be named Nagaland within the Indian Union. They approved the 16 point memorandum. At the same time they passed a significant resolution which runs as follows.

> "The Naga Peoples' Convention further appeals to the Naga people in general and the aggrieved families in particular to extend the same general pardon to the underground people coming overground and also we appeal to all underground Nagas to stop all sorts of violent activities from now on."

A delegation of 15 members of the NPC went to New Delhi in July 1960 and submitted the memorandum to the Ministry of External Affairs and after discussion presented the final version. Prime Minister Nehru agreed to the 16-point agreement with the NPC. He announced on 1st August 1960 in Parliament that a new State to be called Nagaland would be established comprising the NHTA.[32] The NHTA was converted into a full fledged State of Nagaland which was inaugurated on 1st December, 1963 by President S. Radhakrishnan.

Cessation of Operation (6th September, 1964)

Prime Minister Nehru was intent on a negotiated settlement with the Federal Government of Nagaland. An Agreement on the cessation of operation between Indian Army and Naga Army was announced on 6th September 1964. However unfortunately Prime Minister Nehru passed away on 27th May 1964 before the announcement of the agreement. The negotiation between the two parties continued for seven years (1964-1971). The talk between the Government of India and Federal Government of Nagaland was held at the Prime Ministers' level but it broke down on issue of sovereignty of Nagaland. After the breakdown of the negotiation, there was military pressure on the Naga rebels and Governor L.P. Singh succeeded in persuading half a dozen prominent Naga leaders to sign an accord between them and the Government of India. According to this accord,

> "The representative of the underground organization conveyed the decision, of their own volition, to accept, without condition the Constitution of India."

This accord created a split within the Naga movement. A.Z. Phizo, President of the NNC refused to endorse peace accord in public. Three leaders of the NNC namely, Isak Swu, Foreign Secretary, S.S. Khaplang of Eastern Nagas and Thuingaleng Muivah, General Secretary of NNC broke away from NNC to form a new organization named National Socialist Council of Nagaland (NSCN) in 1980.

The Manifesto of the NSCN

The National Socialist Council of Nagaland made a political statement on the Naga nationalism and its plan for carrying out the Naga revolution in form of a manifesto dated January 1980. The NSCN condemned the NNC and declared the following:

a. ***"National existence***

We stand for the unquestionable sovereign right of the Naga people over every inch of Nagaland whatever it may be and admit of no other existence whatever.

b. ***Political institution***

We stand for the principle of people's supremacy, that is, the dictatorship of the people through the National Socialist council and the practice of Democracy within the organization.

c. ***Economic system***

We stand for Socialism. Because it is the only social and economic system that does away with exploitation and ensures fair equality to all the people.

d. ***Religion***

We stand for the faith in God and the salvation of mankind in Jesus, the Christ, alone, that is '**Nagaland for Christ**'. However, the individual freedom of religion shall be safeguarded and the imposition of this faith on others is strictly forbidden.

e. ***Means***

We rule out the illusion of saving Nagaland through peaceful means. It is arms and arms alone that will save our nation and ensure freedom to the people.

f. ***Self-reliance and the Policy of United Front***

We stand for the practice of the principle of self-reliance and for the policy of United Front with all the forces that can be united with [(33)]".

Very soon the NSCN was split into two factions: NSCN led by Isak Swu and Th. Muivah which came to be known as NSCN (IM) and the other was led by S.S. Khaplang which came to be known as NSCN (K). The NSCN established a government named the Government of People's Republic of Nagaland (GPRN) which was also split into two. Three factions were in existence in middle of 1980s: NNC and Federal Government of Nagaland run by it, NSCN (IM) and NSCN (K) which were running the two factions of the GPRN. The NSCN (IM) made a Ceasefire Agreement with the Government of India signed on 25 July 1997 to be effective from the next 1st August. The ceasefire was later on declared to be of an indefinite duration and ground rules for the ceasefire were approved. Series of talks between Government of India and NSCN (IM) were carried out in foreign countries and in India. It is an ongoing peace talk.

Bedrock of Naga Society

Amidst the divergent political view expressed by the revolutionaries that Nagas have always been a nation, a political pamphlet entitled 'Bedrock of Naga Society' was published in the summer of 2000 A.D. by the ruling Nagaland Congress Party which was presumably the brainchild of Nagaland's Chief Minister, S.C. Jamir. This pamphlet was a political testament of those leaders who accepted the 16-point agreement of 1960 and the establishment of the Statehood of Nagaland within India is a consequence of this agreement. This pamphlet was a negative reply to the idea of the Nagas being an independent political entity from time immemorial. The pamphlet asked, "where we really an independent nation"? This statement quoted from the pamphlet represented the view of the Nagas who accepted Indian Constitution, statehood within the Indian Union and Indian democracy and Indian citizenship. The pamphlet observes,

> "The stark and inescapable truth is that neither did we have a definite and unified political structure and nor did we exist as a nation. We were actually a group of heterogeneous, primitive and diverse tribes living in far-flung villages that had very little in common and negligible contact with each other...Each village was practically an entity in itself. The main 'contact' between villages was through the savage practice of headhunting. Mutual suspicion and distrust was rife. Internecine warfare was the order of the day. There was no trust or interaction between different tribes. In these circumstances, the question of a unified 'Naga nation' did not arise. No one can dispute these historical truths. There is enough documentation recorded by the British administrators some as late as the 19th century, which gives the correct picture as it existed. One cannot ignore such historical evidence and rely on emotional outburst alone."

The Nagas continue to claim that they were an independent nation till the British conquered them. Did they have a boundary for their nation? As late as the 1940s, when British rule was almost over, large parts of today's Nagaland did not even exist on their maps. Instead of showing villages the maps showed large blank white spaces with the words "Unadministered and Unsurveyed". Did they have a ruler or a Government? The writ of a village chief did not extend beyond his village. Did they have a capital city where the Government sat? The British deputy Commissioner sat at Kohima out of convenience. Was this the capital of the independent Naga nation that they claim existed before the British? Did they have a currency or a coinage like other kingdoms or nations? Did the Nagas have common laws, rule and regulations for their nation as a whole? Did they have an administrative apparatus to look after the welfare of the people? Did the Nagas have roads that linked the nation?...The plain fact is that they never existed as an independent, unified nation at any time in their history. Yes, each village existed independently, but is that the equivalent of a Naga Nation? Even the names Naga or Angami or Ao or Sema or Chang were unknown. They called people of different tribes by other names.[34]

This pamphlet created an enormous controversy among the Nagas. It was condemned by the NSCN (IM) group which also condemned the 16 point agreement of 1960. There was a debate among the political, social and civil society groups. The Naga Peoples' Movement for Human Rights (NPMHR) went to the extent of deploring it as a distortion of Naga history. The contents of the pamphlet was a reminder of the State of Naga society before the establishment of any organized administration among them. True, as the Naga leaders always claimed that Naga Village Society was always a living entity. The British administration had provided the political organization of the Nagas. It would be erroneous to ignore the history of the Nagas during the British rule and that of pre 1960 history. The pamphlet also created a lot of interest among Indian political observers. Sanjib Barua remarked,

> "Bedrock is undoubtedly a political document with the signature of the Congress Party and former Chief Minister Jamir who was known to be firmly opposed to the NSCN (IM) leader, Muivah. Yet its broader significance should not be under estimated. The lines between independentist and integrationist factions in Naga politics have always been blurred; in that sense this intervention is part of a debate among the Naga nationalists. It is rare in the history of the

> practice of nationalism for a constructionist position of a group's identity to be presented with such candour."[35]

IV

The fallout of Naga Movement in Manipur

Since Manipur has a sizeable population of the Nagas living in the State, the Naga movement started in Naga Hills at the time of India's independence was also felt in Manipur. The first Naga movement for secession from Manipur was started by a Mao Naga leader named Athikho Daiho who started the Naga National League in 1948. He started a movement of the Mao Nagas for solidarity and independence. This movement was suppressed by the government of Manipur and the leaders were jailed. A. Daiho participated in the electoral politics in Manipur in the post colonial period. The Naga Voluntary Plebiscite of 1951 and the boycott of elections in Naga Hills did not have much effect on the Nagas of Manipur. The outbreak of the hostilities between the Naga Home Guards and the Indian Security Forces covered Naga areas of Manipur. The underground Nagas took shelter in Manipur Naga areas. Indian military operations were directed in the Naga areas also. The organization of Naga Peoples' Convention (1957-60) attracted the attention of the Naga leaders of Manipur. They closely followed the process of formation of Union Territory of NHTA and the adoption 16-point memorandum by the NPC which included one point which decided that the Nagas of contiguous areas might join the new State of Nagaland.

Manipur Naga Council (1960)

The Manipur Naga Council (MNC) was established by pro NNC Naga leaders of Manipur under the leadership of one Naga M.P. from Manipur, R. Suisa and his colleague Z. Ramyo joined the NNC. The Manipur Naga Council boycotted the General Election of 1962 responding to the call of the underground Nagas to boycott the Indian election. This group formed the core of the Naga Nationalists of Manipur who wanted secession from Manipur and India. When the agreement for the secession of operation was signed in 1964, three sub divisions of Manipur were included in the area of its operation: sub division of Tamenglong, Mao Maram and Ukhrul and peace observer groups operated in Naga areas of Manipur fro maintenance of peace. During this period of secession of operation, many Naga youths joined the NNC. R. Suisa the M.P. joined the NNC, Th. Muivah became General Secretary of NNC and Z. Ramyo who was made the Home Secretary of the Federal Government of Nagaland became a very prominent spokesman of the Naga cause. He joined the delegation in the Naga talks with the Government of India. As well known the India Naga talks did not produce any fruitful settlement and due to the military pressure of the Government of India several Naga leaders signed the controversial Shillong Accord. Z. Ramyo was a signatory of the accord. Meanwhile Th. Muivah recruited a large number of Naga youth from Manipur to join the Naga army. He himself led a number of Naga rebels to China for military training. Against the Shillong Accord the National Socialist Council of Nagaland was formed. There were clashes between the NSCN and the Federal Government of Nagaland.

When the ceasefire between NSCN (IM) and Government of India was signed in July 1997, the Government of Manipur and many political and civil society organizations expressed their strong opinion that the ceasefire should not be extended to Manipur. Manipur Assembly passed several resolutions against the extension of the ceasefire. They also stood for the territorial integrity of Manipur. National political parties of India including the Indian National Congress and the Bharatya Janta Party made a firm decision for the preservation of the unity and integrity of the States in north east India. However, in June 2001 the Government of India agreed the India-Naga ceasefire would have no territorial limit. There was a hue and cry against this declaration particularly in Manipur. This public outburst compelled the Government of India to revoke declaration on the non territorial limit of the ceasefire. Manipur had become a great factor in the talk between Government of India and the Nagas. There was also further complication due to the existence of several militant outfits of the Meiteis in Manipur. They were unanimously opposed to integration of Naga areas of Manipur into the State of Nagaland or any Naga State. This stalemate continues.

V

The Kuki Aspiration for a Homeland

Kukis or Kuki-Chins constitute a small section of the population of Manipur. There were three factions among these groups: the Kuki proper represented by Kuki National Assembly, Kuki National Front (KNF) and other militant Kuki outfits, the second was the Paites represented by the Paite National Council (PNC) and militant outfits like Zomi Revolutinary Army and the Hmars represented by the Hmar National Union. In mid 1960s the Kukis joined the Mizos in the rebellion organized by Laldenga. This Kuki-Mizo alliance created an atmosphere for the integration of Kuki inhabited areas of Manipur to Mizoram. However after the conclusion of Laldenga-Rajiv Gandhi Accord which provided the statehood for Mizoram, the Kukis were confined in Manipur in their political movement. However various factions of the Kuki militants worked for solidarity and unity of Manipur ranging from the formation of Kuki State or district or administrative unit which were expressed through the demand for a homeland in Manipur State. The Paites were opposed to Mizo and Kuki rebellion. The Hmars who had difference with the Kukis were confined to demand for integration of Hmar inhabited areas in Mizoram, Manipur and Assam into administrative units. The first political demand of the Kukis was expressed by the Kuki National Assembly in January 1960. They submitted a memorandum for a demand of a Kuki State to the Prime Minister of India. The memorandum among others mentions,

> "...exercising their right to enjoy 'self determination' to determine their own political destiny, the Kuki National Assembly, India therefore in this general meeting have thereby resolved while affirming its solidarity with the rest of the country, to make a just and strong demand to the Government of India for the

> immediate establishment of the Kuki State, unification of all contiguous areas now under the habitation of Kukis in India and to pursue their demand to its final end."[36]

The demand for Kuki State provided an umbrella for the expression of aspiration of the Kukis for a homeland. Several organizations both overground and underground sprang up. Some of them are the Kuki National Front (KNF), Kuki National Army (KNA), Kuki National Organization (KNO), United Kuki Liberation Front (UKLF), etc. The most vociferous demand of the Kukis was the formation of the Sadar Hills District within Manipur.

Kuki Naga Conflict

An aspect of Naga movement in Manipur was its conflict against the Kukis who were scattered throughout Manipur hills. During the colonial period, there were frequent conflicts between the Nagas and the Kukis. In 1993, an ethnic conflict between these two groups led to open violence between them. There were allegations of ethnic cleansing among them. After nearly seven years of conflict due to the self restraint of the NSCN (IM) leadership and KNF leaders, the conflict was subsided. When the Kuki-Naga Conflict was continuing, a section of the Paites and the Kukis came into open clash in southern district of Manipur. Somehow the Government of Manipur under the Chief Ministership of W. Nipamacha Singh intervened and solved the hostility between the two.

In Manipur the Naga movement which was opposed by Meiteis who are determined to preserve the territorial integrity of their ancient kingdom and where the Kukis are aspiring for a homeland, immediate solution of these conflicts and tensions is not foreseen. But every problem will have a solution and the Indian statesmanship with their wisdom and resources is expected to provide lasting resolutions.

NOTES

1. Petersen, William, Concepts of Ethnicity in the selections from the Harvard *Encyclopedia of American Ethnic Groups*, Harvard University Press, 1980.

2. Connor, Walker, wrote 9 essays which were published in his Ethnonationalism: *The Quest for Understanding*, Princeton University Press, Princeton, New Jersey, 1984. In 2001, he wrote another paper entitled "In lieu of conclusion: Ethnonationalism and Tomorrow's World Map" which was the key note address of an international seminar on "*Ethnic Dimensions in International Politics*" at the Guru Nanak Dev University, Amritsar published in Gurnam Singh edited Ethno-nationalism and Emerging World (Dis) Order, New Delhi, 2002.

3. Connor, Walker, *In lieu of conclusion: Ethnonationalism and Tomorrow's World Map.* In Gurnam Singh edited, *op cit,* pp. 380-382.

4. Connor, Walker, Ethnonationalism, *op cit,* p. 11.

5. Conversi, Daniele, Conceptualizing Nationalism: An Introduction to walker Connor's Work, quoted in Sanjib Baruah's Ethnonationalism in India, Oxford University Press, 2010, p. 16

6. Connor, Walker, in Gurnam Singh, *op cit,* p. 381.

7. Smith, Anthony D. *The Ethnic Revival*, Cambridge University press, 1981, pp. 58-61.

8. Baruah, Sanjib, (ed), *Ethnonationalism in India: A Reader, An Introduction*, p.1, Oxford University Press, New Delhi, 2010

9. *Ibid.*

10. Rothschild, Joseph, *Ethnopolitics: A Conceptual Framework*, Columbia University Press, New York, 1981.

11. Parratt, Saroj Nalini Arambam, *Regionalism in Manipur*: An attempt at analyzing the causes of Meitei insurgency movement in Collected papers on history and culture of Manipur, Imphal, 2010, pp. 219 - 240. Sanajaoba, N. *Genesis of insurgency in Manipur Past and Present*, Vol.I, New Delhi, 1988, pp. 245 – 290. Phanjoubam, Tarapot (1993), *Insurgency Movement in North Eastern India.*

12. Singh, N. Joykumar, *Revolutionary Movements in Manipur*, New Delhi, 2005.

13. Kamei, Gangmumei, in the foreword to N. Joykumar Singh's work, p. vi.
14. Lenin, *State and Revolution in Collected Works*, Vol. 33, Moscow, 1973, p. 110.
15. Kamei, Gangmumei, Recurrence of Historical Forces: Insurgency in Manipur, 1891 in *On History and Historiography of Manipur*, New Delhi, 2002, pp. 138-139.
16. See Chapters 15 and 19 of this book for more elucidation
17. Singh, N. Joykumar, *op cit,* Genesis of the Movements, pp. 26-53 and Saroj Nalini Arambam Parratt, op cit, pp. 225-231.
18. Singh, See Karam Manimohan, *Hijam Irabot Singh and Political movements in Manipur*, Delhi, 1989 and N. Lokendra Singh, *op cit*, Appendix on Manipur Conspiracy Case, 1952
19. Singh, N. Joykumar *op cit,* p. 59. He was the first scholar who did a detailed study of the exploits of the Meitei State Committee based on personal interviews with former members of the committee and police reports.
20. Constantine, R. *Manipur: Maid of the Mountains*, 1981, p. 89.
21. Singh, N. Joykumar, *op cit,* p. 63.
22. Criminal Miscellaneous Petition. Quoted in N. Joykumar Singh, *op cit,* p. 72.
23. Singh, N. Joykumar, *op cit,* p. 76.
24. The names of the Lhasa bound Manipuri youths were (1) Kabichandra, (2) Indrajit, (3) N. Nilamani, (4) Biramangol, (5) N. Rajen Achouba, (6) Chirom Ranjit, (7) Rajen Macha, (8) S. Temba, (9) Thoudam Kunjabihari, (10) Manikanta, (11) Chaobhal, (12) W. brojen Singh, (13) Amumacha, (14) Kh. Khaba, (15) N. Thoiba, (16) Loya, (17) Surjaboro, (18) Chaoba, (19) Kulla, (20) N. Biseshwor
25. In 2006, the PREPAK was again reunited. However another faction led by Defence Secretary Chinglenba Mangang split of to form the United Peoples' Party of Kangleipak (UPPK).
26. Elwin, Verrier, *Nagaland*, Reprint 1997, Delhi, pp. 71-72.

27. Memorandum of the case of the Naga people for self-determination and an APPEAL to H.M.G. and the Government of India submitted by NNC to Viceroy Louis Lord Mountbatten on 20th February 1947 quoted in Asoso Yonuo, Nagas Struggle Against British Rule etc., 1982, Delhi, pp. 132-136.

28. The cable to Secretary General, United Nations dated 14th August, 1947 reads thus:

    To The Secretary General, United Nations,

    Benign Excellency,

    *Kindly put on Record that Nagas will be Independent

    *Discussion with India are being carried on to that effect

    *Nagas do not accept Indian Constitution

    *The Right of the people must prevail regardless of size

    *Naga National Council

    Note (This message was acknowledged by UN and record is both in UN and NNC's files). V.K. Nuh (compiled) The Naga Chronicle, op cit, p.115.

29. *The Naga Chronicle*, Naga Voluntary Plebiscite, pp. 116-133.

30. Verrier Elwin, *op cit,* p. 65.

31. *Ibid.*

32. The text of the 16 point agreement signed between the Naga Peoples' Convention and Prime Minister Jawaharlal Nehru in July, 1960 is published in most of the standard works on the Naga politics. The text for this work is reproduced from V.K. Nuh, The Naga Chronicle, 2002, Shillong, pp. 195-198

33. The Manifesto is reproduced from Anuradha Dutta and Ratna Bhuyan (ed), *Genesis of Conflict and Peace: Understanding Northeast India views and reviews,* Delhi, 2007, pp. 506-509.

34. Nagaland Pradesh Congress Committee (NPCC), *Bedrock of Naga Society*, Kohima, June 2000, pp. 6-8.

35. Barua, Sanjib, Confronting Constructionism: ending the Naga war in his Ethnonationalism in India, op cit, pp. 239-262. Sanjib Barua divided

the Naga nationalist into two groups, independentist and integrationist. The first stood for the independence of Nagas and the latter stands for the integration of all the Nagas in India and Burma into a political State either Nagaland in India or Nagalim in general.

36. Gangte, T.S. Problems of Ethnicity and Identity in contemporary Manipur: a scenario in Manipur hill, published by Centre for Ethnic and Identity Studies, Imphal, 2008, pp. 1-22. Please see also T.S. Gangte, Land problem and ethnic tension in northeast India with special reference to Manipur, in Understanding Kuki since primordial times edited by Aheibam Koireng Singh and Priyadarshini M. Gangte, New Delhi, 2010

REFERENCES

Alemchiba, M. *A brief history of Nagaland*, Kohima, 1965.

Brass, Paul, *Ethnicity and Nationalism*, New Delhi, 1991.

Jassal, R.S. *Militancy and Conflict Resolution in Manipur*, New Delhi, 2011.

Laishram, Dhanabir, *et al.*, *The Stitch: Ethnicty, Insurgency and Development in Manipur*, New Delhi, 2009.

Pakem, B. (ed), *Insurgency in North East India*, New Delhi, 1997.

Pakem, B. (ed), *Nationality, Ethnicity and Cultural Identity in North East India*, Delhi, 2005.

Parratt, John, *Wounded Land,* New Delhi, 2005.

Singh, Aheibam Koireng, *Ethnicity and Inter-community conflicts*, New Delhi, 2008.

Sema, Hokishe, *Emergence of Nagaland*, New Delhi, 1986.

Tarapot Phanjoubam, *Bleeding Manipur*, New Delhi, 1998

Verghese, B.G. *India: North East Resurgent*, Delhi, 1996.

APPENDIX

Names of Meitei militant outfits in Manipur

Sl.No	*Name of outfit*	*Strength*	*Area of Operation*
1	PLA-RPF	1500	Imphal, Bishnupur and Thoubal
2	UNLF (now MPLF)	1000	Imphal, Bishnupur and Chandel
3	PREPAK(Red Army)	200	Imphal, Bishnupur and parts of Chandel
4	KCP	100	Thoubal and Imphal districts
5	KCP (Noyon)	370 in all	
6	KCP (Lamphel)		
7	KCP (Lallhumba)		
8	KCP (MC)		
9	KCP (VC)		
10	KCP (L. Khuman)		
11	KCP (MTF)		
12	KCP (Nongdren Khomba)		
13	KCP (MC. Tongaba)		
14	KCP (Maoist)		
15	KYKL (O)	170	Bishnupur, Imphal districts
16	KYKL (T)	50	Imphal and Thoubal district
17	KYKL (MDF)		
18	KDF (Kangleipak D. Force)		
19	UPPK (United Peoples' Party of Kangleipak)		
20	UKLA (MC)		
21	KCP (Nando)		
22	KCP (Nganba)		
23	PREPAK (VC)		
24	PREPAK (GS)		

Kuki Outfits of Manipur

Sl.No	Name of outfit	Strength	Area of Operation
1	UKLF (United Kuki Liberation Front)	50	Chandel, Moreh, Tengnoupal
2	KNA/KNO	200	Parts of Chandel, Churachandpur and some influence in Sadar Hills
3	KNF (MC)	250	Senapati, Churachandpur (with ZRA) and Sadar Hills
4	KNF (PC)	20	Jiribam, Sadar Hills
5	KNF (S)		
6	ZRA/ UPF	400	Churachandpur
7	HPC (D)	60	Vangai range, Jiribam
8	HRF	40	Churachandpur
9	HNA (Hmar National Army)		
10	KRA (Kuki Revolutionary Army)	50	Sadar Hills
11	CKRF (Chin Kuki Revolutionary Front)		

Naga Outfits of Manipur

Sl.No	Name of outfit	Strength	Area of Operation
1	NSCN (IM)	800	Ukhrul, Senapati, Tamenglong
2	NSCN (K)	300	Ukhrul, Senapati, Tamenglong
3	NNC (Adino)		
4	MNRF	50	South Ukhrul
5	NNC (Khadao)	100	
6	ZUF (Zeliangrong United Front)		
7	UNPC (United Nagas Peoples' Convention)	18	
8	USRA (United Socialist Revolutionary Army)		
9	PULF (Peoples' United Liberation Front) of the Muslim under NSCN (IM) protege	400	Thoubal, Dimapur

Source: R.S. Jassal, *Militancy and Conflict Resolution in Manipur*, New Delhi, 2011, Table 1. Intrinsic Conflict quoting official sources, pp. 70-72.

Bibliography

Administrative reports of Manipur from 1891-1946.

Alemchiba, M. *A brief history of Nagaland*, Kohima, 1965.

Barnes, H.E. *A History of Historical Writings,* New York, 1963.

Bloch, Marc, *Historian's Craft*, London, 1953.

————, *The Feudal Society* Vol I & II, London, 1939.

Brass, Paul, *Ethnicity and Nationalism*, New Delhi, 1991.

Braudel, Ferdinald, *On History*, London, 1986.

Brown, R. *A Statistical Account of Manipur*, Calcutta, 1874.

Bury, J.B. *The Idea of Progress: an enquiry into its origin and growth*, New York, 1954.

Carr, E.H. *What is History?* London, 1962.

Chandrasekhar, Kh. (Ed): *Loiyamba Shilyen*, Imphal, 1984..

Collingwood, R.G. *The Idea of History*, London, 1945.

Dena, Lal. *Christian Missions and Colonialism*, Shillong, 1986.

Downs, F.S. *The Mighty Works of God*, Gauhati, 1980.

Dun, E.W. *Gazetteer of Manipur*, Shimla, 1886.

Evans, E.W. (Ed), *Methods and Principles of Colonial Administration*, London, 1950.

Furnivall, F.S. *Colonial Policy and Practice*, London, 1948.

Gardiner, Patrick, *Theories of History*, New York, 1969.

Goel, Dharmendra, *Philosophy of History*, Delhi, 1967.

Hamilton, Paul, *Historicism*, Routledge, London, 1996.

Hegel, W.G.F. *Lectures on the Philosophy of World History* (1822-1830), London, 1975.

Higgins, J.C. : *Notes on Meithei (Manipuri) Beliefs and Customs*, Edited by John Parrat, Imphal, 1998.

Hobsbawm, Eric, *On History*, London, 1997.

Hodson, T.C. *The Meitheis*, London, 1908.

International Encyclopedia of Social Science: Vol V, 1972 on Feudalism, Joshua Prawar and Samuel N Eisenstadt, pp 393-402.

Jassal, R.S. *Militancy and Conflict Resolution in Manipur*, New Delhi, 2011.

Johnstone, James: *My Experience in Manipur and Naga Hills*, London, 1896.

Kamei, Gangmumei : *A History of Manipur: A Pre-Colonial Period*, Vol. I, National Publishing House, New Delhi, 1991 and 2004 Edn.

————, *On History and Historiography of Manipur*, Delhi, 2006.

————, *Rajkumar Sanahal Singh*, B.Com, Memorial Lecture, Maharaj Sir Churachand Singh (1891-1941) in Modern Period of Manipur History, organised by Manipuri Sahitya Parishad, Imphal, 2006

————, From Tribalism to Feudalism: Evolution of the Meitei State in Pre-Colonial Manipur, *Professor H.K. Barpujari, Endowment Lecture 2009* published by North Eastern India History Association, Shillong, 2010.

————, *Presidential Address: State Formation in North East India: A review,* North East India History Association 1986, Kohima Session.

Khelchandra , N. (Edn): *Phamlon, Manipur* Sahitya Parishad, Imphal, 1997.

Kosambi, D.D. *An Introduction to the study of Indian History*, Bombay, 1975, 1988 (Revd Edn).

Laishram, Dhanabir, *et al., The Stitch: Ethnicty, Insurgency and Development in Manipur*, New Delhi, 2009.

Lal Dena (ed), *William Pettigrew: A Centenary Tribute*, Published by Ashok Tipnis, Imphal, 1996

Leontyev, L. *Pre-Capitalist Modes of Production n Political Economy*, 1972, Moscow.

Levi-Strauss, Claude, *Structural Anthropology*, London, 1968

Luikham, T. *A short history of Manipur Baptist Christian*, Calcutta, 1948.

MacKenzie, Alexander: *A History of Relation of the Hill Tribes with the Government of all North Eastern Frontier of Bengal*, 1884, Calcutta (relevant portion).

McCulloch, W. *An Account of Valley of Munnipore,* Calcutta, 1859.

Mclallan, David: *Karl Marx, Selected Writings*, Oxford University Press, 1977, 2000 (2nd Edn), 2001 (Reprint).

Misra, B.B. *Administrative History of India 1834-1947*, Oxford University Press, New Delhi, 1970.

Mukhia, Harbans : *The Feudal Debate*, 1999, Delhi.

Neill, Stephen, *Colonialism and Christian Mission*, London, 1966.

Ningthougi chahi yangkhei subagi wari (Story of fifty years of the King) published on the occasion of Golden Jubilee celebration of Maharaj Sir Churachand Singh, Imphal, 1941.

Pakem, B. (ed), *Insurgency in North East India*, New Delhi, 1997.

————, (ed), *Nationality, Ethnicity and Cultural Identity in North East India*, Delhi, 2005.

Parratt explained the British rule in Manipur as a combination of British colonialism, feudalism of Raja Churachand Singh and Brahminism of Manipuri Hindus.

Parratt, John, *Wounded Land,* New Delhi, 2005.

————, , *The Wounded Land: Politics and Identity in Modern Manipur*, New Delhi, 2005.

Pettigrew, William, *Twentyfive Years. 1897-1922*, Ukhrul Mission School, 1922.

Raunier, Rene, *Sociology of Colonies*, Vol.I, Routledge and Kegan Paul, London, 1948.

Resolutions of the Manipur State Durbar (1907-1946).

Roy, Singh, *History of Manipur*, Calcutta 1958.

Roy, J. *A History of Manipur*, Calcutta, 1958.

Sema, Hokishe, *Emergence of Nagaland*, New Delhi, 1986.

Sen, S.P. (ed.), *Historians and Historiography of Modern India*, Calcutta, 1973.

Sharma, Nandalal: *Meitrabak*, Imphal, 1960.

Sharma, R.S. *Indian Feudalism*, 1965, 1980 (Revd Edn).

————, *Material Culture and Social Formation in Ancient India*, Macmillan, Delhi, 1983, 2000 (Reprint).

————, *Perspective to Social and Economic History of Early India*, 1983, 1995 (Revd Edn).

Singh, Aheibam Koireng, *Ethnicity and Inter-community conflicts*, New Delhi, 2008.

Singh, Ch. Manihar (Ed): *Naothingkhong Phambal Kaba* (in English tranaslation), Imphal, 1986.

Singh, K. Manimohan, *Christian Missionary Movement in Manipur*, Imphal, 1990.

Singh, L. Chandramani: *Manipur Itihas* (in Manipuri) Imphal, 1970.

Singh, L. Iboongohal: *An Introduction to Manipur*, Imphal, 1960.

Singh, L.M.I. and Pandit N Khelchandra Singh: *The Cheitharol Kumbaba*, 1st Edn, 1967.

Singh, N. Ibobi: *The Manipur Administration (1709-1907),* Imphal, 1976, 2003 (Reprint).

Singh, N. Joykumar, *Colonialism to Democracy: A History of Manipur from 1819-1972*, 2002.

————, *From Colonialism to Democracy, A Modern History of Manipur*, Guwahati.

Singh, N. Lokendra *Unquiet Valley*, 1998.

Singh, N. Lokendra: *Unquiet Valley,* Mittal Publications, New Delhi, 1996.

Singh, R.K. Jhalajit, *A Short History of Manipur*, Imphal, 1965.

————, *A Short History of Manipur*, Imphal, 1965.

Singh, R.K. Sanahal, *Manipur Itihas*, Imphal 1947.

————, *Manipur Itihas*, Imphal, 1947.

Spengler, Oswald, *The Decline of the West*, London, 1959.

Stranse-Hupe and Harry W. Hozard, *Ideas of Colonialism*, New York, 1958.

Subramaniam, N. *Historiography*, Madras, 1974.

Tarapot Phanjoubam, *Bleeding Manipur*, New Delhi, 1998

Thakur, V.K. *Historiography of Indian Feudalism towards a Model of Early Medieval Indian Economy*, Delhi, 1989.

Thapar, Romila, *History & Beyond*, Oxford University Press, 2010.

Verghese, B.G. *India: North East Resurgent*, Delhi, 1996.

Yaima, Kh. (Ed): *Pakhangba Phambal*, Imphal, 1967.

Index